DR LYDIA MOUSSA

NAVIGATING THE CHAOS OF
CHANGE

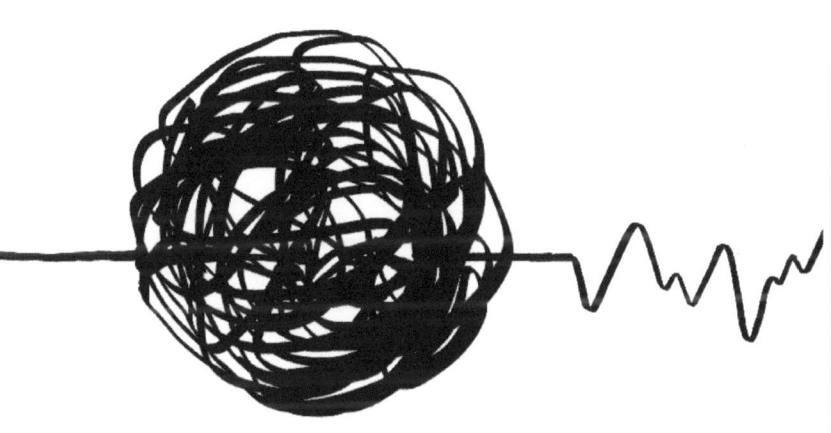

Using a dynamic navigation system
The 6E Change Facilitation Framework

Copyright © 2022 Lydia Moussa

All rights reserved. No part of this publication may be reproduced, distributed, or transmitted in any form or by any means, including photocopying, recording, or other electronic or mechanical methods, without the prior written permission of the publisher, except in the case of brief quotations embodied in critical reviews and certain other noncommercial uses permitted by copyright law. For permission requests, write to the publisher, addressed "Attention: Permissions Coordinator," at the address below.

Moussa, Lydia
Navigating the Chaos of Change
ISBN: 978-0-6453458-2-7

Cover and book design by Sh8peshifters
Illustrations by Sh8peshifters

Published by Project Midnight
First printing edition
Sydney, Australia

Contents

Acknowledgement	1
Preface	3
Introduction	5
Part I Humans & Change	9
Chapter 1: Brain Battles	11
Battles, bribes and bad-mouthing	13
The 'ta-da' moment	18
Choosing death over change	22
Chapter 2: Change Chaos	27
It takes a plague	29
The pendulum of chaos	34
The complexity of humans	38
Part II Changing Change	43
Chapter 3: Time for a change in change	45
From linear to dynamic	47
From divide to combine	52
From managing to facilitating	57
Chapter 4: A Transformation Journey	63
The messy cupboard of change	65
No silver bullet	71
A dynamic change framework	75

Part III 3E's for Implementation — 83

Chapter 5: Explore Change Factors — 85
- Factors far and wide — 87
- Rebellion, rubbish and ramifications — 93
- Global and cultural factors — 98

Chapter 6: Establish Change Strategies — 105
- Pain-killer or antibiotic? — 107
- Global visions to granular measures — 111
- Walls versus boundaries — 115

Chapter 7: Evaluate Change Progress — 121
- Why not both? — 123
- E-value-ation — 128
- Perfection versus iteration — 134

Part IV 3E's for Adoption — 141

Chapter 8: Engage Stakeholders during the change — 143
- Building and bridging the vision — 145
- The root of all evil — 149
- Easy to break, hard to rebuild — 155

Chapter 9: Empower stakeholders to plan for change — 161
- Many members - one organisational body — 163
- From power to empower — 168
- We are the champions — 174

Chapter 10: Equip stakeholders with change capabilities **181**

Skills, sleep and smartboards 183
Driving the learning journey 189
Same same but different 194

Part V The 6E Change Facilitation Framework **201**

Chapter 11: The Change Journey **203**

Nancy & Adam - Revisited 205
The 6E's in practice 209
The whole picture 216

References **224**

Acknowledgement

To my father - Michel, thank you for embedding deep-rooted values, whilst teaching me how to be adaptable and navigate change in my life. To my mother - Mona, thank you for showing me what it means to pursue opportunities no matter the unknown. To my sisters - Engy and Sandra, thank you for always being there as a guiding compass to where my roots lie and what to value most in life.

To my husband - Andrew, you are a living example of what it means to put people at the centre of everything you do. Your constant love, encouragement and support make you an exceptional role model for our children and change agent at work. I love you and am so blessed to be by your side through the chaotic journey of life.

To my children - Elaria and Adam, I love you dearly. You are my motivation. I am so grateful that God has granted us two incredible children who are wise beyond their years and teach us what it means to love and hope through all the chaos.

To my academic mentor - Victoria, thank you for your guidance through my research journey, pushing me to look deeper at the data and challenge the status quo.

To my publishers and illustrators - Alan and Diana from Sh8peshifters, you've been there from the beginning of my journey; your work is incredible - thank you.

To my family, friends and Coptic Community – thank you for being my safety net and home no matter the chaos.

To a loving and gracious God, the One who gives me peace and comfort through all the chaos. I am truly blessed and eternally grateful.

Preface

"Be like a tree, having a solid trunk and deep roots, yet flexible branches, swaying with the changing wind without breaking."

Michel Guirguis (my father)

On a summer afternoon in 1996, my parents announced the decision for our family to take the most significant leap of faith we have ever taken. A leap so big, it would land us halfway across the world onto a tiny island we had never heard of - New Zealand, and subsequently, change the course of our lives.

At ten years of age, this was the first major change in my young life, but certainly not the last. Our family moved from Egypt to New Zealand and then Australia, during which I attended seven different schools. Change became the one constant part of my life, sometimes by choice, other times by necessity. Whether friend or foe, it has always been present and continuously shaped the person I have become.

All this change left some scars at the start, but when I began to view it differently, it brought about unexpected things. Each school added something different; the ability to fit in, a love for sport, a passion for public speaking, dealing with rejection and bullies, leadership opportunities and friendships. Moving countries made me appreciate diversity, culture, languages and culinary experiences. Later on, changes in my career helped me build skills like; strategy, collaboration, conflict resolution, training and leadership engagement. Combined, all the changes in my life taught me a critical skill- adaptability.

Change may come as a gentle breeze, welcomed rain during a drought, an exciting whirlwind or a devastating hurricane. Whatever the change, we must decide whether to avoid, reject and despise it or to seek, embrace and ultimately learn to navigate its chaos.

Since 2011, I have dedicated my life to change - completing my PhD on how to implement it, understanding how it affects people, working with teams to navigate it, and educating MBA students and organisations on understanding it. This does not mean I have it completely figured out. Every day, I learn something new; every project challenges and pushes me to think differently ,and every person facing change gives me greater insight into its effects.

While I continue to adapt and grow in this ever-evolving change landscape, I hold steadfast to the mantra that my father instilled in me from a young age.

'Be like a tree, having a solid trunk and deep roots, yet flexible branches, swaying with the changing wind without breaking.'

This mantra reminds me to stay flexible and adaptable while holding firm to my roots. Not only did it help me through numerous changes, but it also laid a solid foundation for what I have dedicated my life's work to...

Navigating the Chaos of Change.

Introduction

Innovative organisations are more likely to thrive and outperform their competitors. A clear example of this is Apple. The release of the iPod in 2001 took the world by storm and revolutionised how people listened to music. We were finally liberated from the horrid Discman that forced us to carry a folder harbouring numerous scratched music CDs causing poor sound quality. With the iPod, we had hundreds of songs at our fingertips; it played tracks perfectly, and we could pocket the device discreetly. Apple's enormous success continued with innovations such as the iPhone and iPad.

The entertainment industry is another great example. As a teenager, I remember spending hours browsing through a Blockbuster store to find the ideal movie I could rent for a few days. After paying a ridiculous price, I'd usually end up disappointed with my choice and left with a fine due to a late return. While Blockbuster provided a somewhat innovative DVD delivery service, it did not adapt fast enough to capture the streaming subscription market, now dominated by the likes of Netflix.

For organisations to simply survive, the rate at which they need to innovate is higher than ever. An industry's 'clock speed' refers to the measure of its evolutionary life cycle [1]. Put into perspective, the clock speed of organisations has increased by up to five times since 2010. This rapid rate of change can be attributed to three significant factors.

Firstly, increased competitive pressure is pushing organisations to think fast and smart. Using the Blockbuster example, new competitor entrants such as Netflix disrupt industry giants to either pivot or plummet. In the financial sector, banks compete to provide their customers with the most efficient service and seamless experience, enabling them to use their devices to access funds, transfer money instantly and make purchases. Unfortunately, gone are the days when we could tell our kids we didn't have any coins for those annoying carousels in shopping centres. Now my children say, "Mum, just tap your phone".

The second factor is the advancement in knowledge, capabilities and tools. As children in the 1990s, we relied on an encyclopaedia to find information. Over time, this was replaced by the internet - now, on mobile devices, abundant information is literally at our fingertips. At seven years of age, I was learning to construct sentences; now, seven-year-olds are learning to code. As a ten-year-old, I spent hours on my bike throwing leaflets to advertise for my local fish and chip shop. Now, businesses can do their marketing without setting foot outside their office through the power of social media. In 2013, a friend introduced me to the concept of 3D printing, which at the time seemed so foreign. Now it is being used to create appliances, food and even 'organoids' (tiny organs used for medical research).

Thirdly, circumstantial and societal pressures push organisations to adapt quicker than ever. Global climate change has forced organisations to develop more sustainable products that are reusable, biodegradable and recyclable.

We have reusable straws, biodegradable dental floss and recycled toilet paper.

It's also important to note that innovation doesn't just mean 'new' products - it can also improve existing products, systems, processes and even culture.

If adapting to a rapid rate of change is necessary for organisational survival, does that mean people are now more welcoming of change? If so many technologies and innovations are at our fingertips, does that mean people are seeking them and becoming early adopters? Unfortunately, with the increasing rate of change, we are not necessarily seeing an equally increasing adoption rate. On the contrary, change fatigue, resistance, and fear remain prevalent. But why?

People fear the uncertainty and chaos of change when they don't know how to navigate it.

PART I

HUMANS & CHANGE

BRAIN BATTLES 01

 *Resistance is our humanistic survival response to sudden change.*

Dr Lydia Moussa

BATTLES, BRIBES AND BAD-MOUTHING

It was a battle between two strong-willed and persistent individuals. Similar in so many ways, yet the difference - thirty years. Adam looked at the piece of chicken with much scepticism, then looked defiantly at his dad. Will our three-year-old son finally concede and eat the chicken, or will he again continue on the path of resistance that will ultimately lead to a much-dreaded tantrum?

Usually, we are very patient parents (or so we would like to think). Earlier that day, we said we'd make sausages, one of Adam's favourite meals. However, we had forgotten to take the sausages out of the freezer, so last-minute changes had to be made. When Adam saw the chicken on his plate, he immediately entered meltdown mode. He was promised sausages but was given chicken. The battle began. We tried bribing him with the idea of dessert afterwards, but even the incentive of chocolate failed. We attempted the 'stick method' by telling him that if he didn't eat his dinner, he wouldn't get to watch his favourite show the following day - still nothing. We even tried to create a bit of competition between him and his sister to see who could finish their dinner faster - the chicken pieces remained forsaken on his plate.

I know he was only a toddler, and by nature, they can be defiant and unreasonable, but we never experienced this type of resistance from our eldest - Elaria.

We could always convince her of anything using logic and reasoning, even as a toddler. How could two siblings be so different, with one so open to change whilst the other so resistant to it?

As change professionals, my husband, Andrew, and I knew we had to find the key to unlock his resistance. As we sat on the couch that night to reflect on our day, we thought about it from his perspective. What happened that led to his resistance? What usually happens that leads anyone towards resistance?

In reality, it's not just toddlers who seem defiant and unreasonable when it comes to change. Take Nancy (name has been changed for anonymity), who had started a sleep clinic within a medical centre and led it for over ten years. For years she lived and breathed this clinic and knew every patient (even their pets' names).

Nancy came into the room with a creased brow and arms folded tightly. During the entire three-hour meeting, her arms remained crossed. The tension was obvious, but I didn't anticipate how severe the situation had become. How could such a small change have been dealt with so terribly that it escalated to this point?

For the last four years, Nancy had refused to touch a computer as there was always someone with her in the clinic to update the electronic patient records. Three weeks before this meeting, a decision was made to replace her with someone more 'tech savvy' and move Nancy to another position.

How did she initially react to the news of her relocation?

Nancy carried on as if nothing had happened - thinking that management was bluffing and couldn't possibly get rid of the person who started the clinic.

When she realised that her relocation was happening, Nancy decided to act. She threatened the imminent demise of the clinic, began to speak ill of the newcomer in front of customers and even cancelled upcoming patient appointments. When this behaviour was brought to management's attention, she was asked to leave the clinic immediately to commence in her new area. On her way out, she removed her accreditation certificates from the wall, leaving empty frames to make a point that the clinic would be empty without her. At this point, I was asked to come and facilitate a productive discussion.

Before the meeting, management gave me the following brief: "We do not want to let her go, but she is expected to stop this behaviour and work in her new area without causing disruption." I could not help but think that Nancy was only doing what her survival instinct led her to do.

What did Adam and Nancy have in common? They were both victims of poorly navigated change and simply responded based on their survival instincts.

American physiologist, Walter Cannon, recognised that an unconscious and automatic series of fast-acting reactions occur inside the body to help us manage threatening circumstances. His book [2] noted that when predators threaten prey, the prey's bodies release hormones that trigger this survival response.

In humans, these hormones are known as 'cortisol' and 'adrenaline'. Their release helps humans defend themselves in threatening situations by preparing the body to fight or flee. In some circumstances, when we don't know whether to fight or flee, we often freeze.

Figure 1.1 Fight, flee and freeze response to change

When faced with sudden change, human nature also dictates a 'fight', 'flee' or 'freeze' response. Adam and Nancy had chosen to fight.

Adam had a meltdown like any three-year-old would if he was promised something and then not given it, whilst Nancy had an adult-size meltdown when her world was changed very suddenly without her knowledge or input.

What reaction would you have had if you were in Nancy's position? Fight, flee or freeze?

Nancy chose to 'fight' the way she thought was most effective to get her point across. Some in her position might have 'fled' home angrily whilst others could have 'frozen' or become apathetic towards their new role. Everyone responds to sudden change differently, however, the one thing all responses have in common is that they are often unpleasant, destructive and not conducive to positive outcomes.

> **When we feel threatened by a sudden change, our body's instinct is to fight, flee, or freeze- resistance to sudden change is a natural response to this 'threat'.**

THE 'TA-DA' MOMENT

Whilst each person is unique, our core humanistic responses to sudden change tend to follow similar patterns.

Consider the evolution of species - the theory that initially comes to mind is survival of the fittest. Certain animals have been completely eradicated due to environmental change, whilst others thrived through the evolutionary development of their characteristics.

As for human evolution, if there was a particularly long and cold winter, we didn't happen to grow an extra layer of hair but instead created warmer clothing to protect us from the harsh environment. When faced with wild beasts, we gradually developed more advanced weapons to defend ourselves or catch the animals. As Charles Darwin clarified, it was not the strongest who survived but those who learned to adapt to change.

We may no longer be faced with wild beasts, and most of us have what is needed to protect ourselves from the weather, so how does the same concept of adaptation remain relevant today?

I like to use the following analogy when considering the neuroscience of change. Imagine you were on a bush walk and a bear jumped out at you. What would you do?

Your brain will tell you to fight, flee, or freeze. Chances are you would run as fast as your legs can take you, completely forgetting that you are unlikely to outrun a bear.

Now imagine that you are planning a day at the zoo. You may also come face-to-face with a bear, however, this time, you are very much at ease knowing there is an impenetrable glass between you. In both scenarios, you are faced with a bear, so what's the difference?

When we are prepared for a change, our response to it is very different than when it is suddenly thrust upon us, causing our brain to metaphorically 'short-circuit' and default to survival mode.

Fortunately, there is a scientific explanation for this.

Our Basal Ganglia is responsible for our learned behaviours, like brushing our teeth or driving a car. Since the Basal Ganglia helps us with voluntary movements, predicting the same outcome every time, it requires little energy to function.

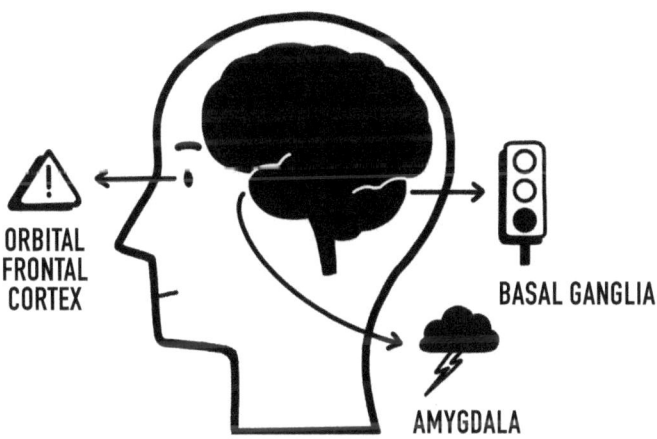

Figure 1.2 The neuroscience that leads to change resistance

When our existing learned behaviours are challenged, the Orbital Frontal Cortex, which supports cognitive decision-making, sends 'error' or 'mismatch' signals to different body parts to respond.

Simultaneously the Amygdala, whose role is to detect threats and activate appropriate fear-related behaviours in response to threatening stimuli, sends a fight, flee, or freeze response, leading to both an 'emotional' and 'irrational' response.

Let's take a typical example in many families: children are blissfully watching TV when a parent suddenly decides it's time to turn it off. In our house, we would typically experience the 'fight' response, shortly followed by 'fleeing' in tears.

This response is typical because while the kids are happily watching their cartoon, their eyes glazed over, the Basal Ganglia is in 'business as usual' mode. When sudden change is thrust upon them, like the TV turning off, their brain sends the error message - "I'm still watching; why is the TV screen black?" Then inevitably, the riots commence.

When this happened too often in our household, Andrew and I discussed strategies to deal with this seemingly irrational but scientifically validated response our children were displaying. We agreed with our three and five-year-olds at the time on the reasonable number of episodes they were allowed to watch. We then handed the little one the remote control (as he usually had the more significant meltdown) and gave him the responsibility of turning it off as soon as they finished the agreed number of episodes.

What was the outcome? Significantly fewer meltdowns, an increased sense of responsibility, induced development of self-control and improved trust between us.

In the workplace, there are many similar examples. Leadership may have known about an upcoming restructure of the organisation, which would inevitably lead to job losses, yet kept it 'secret' to avoid panic. However, when it is announced as a 'ta-da' moment, the outcome is even worse panic. The panic resulting from job terminations instils a sense of fear which manifests in responses of fighting, fleeing or freezing (often referred to as paralysis) [3].

In the face of sudden change, these natural reactions of 'fight, flight or freeze' from employees tend to require responsive action from leadership, including responding to complaints, employee churn, expanding project timeframes and budgets, and other costly and painful interventions.

The intervention I was asked to facilitate with Nancy was the delicate defusion of a bomb on the edge of eruption due to a 'ta-da' moment and poorly navigated change. However, this was a near miss, given there is a direct correlation between poorly implemented changes and high staff turnover [4].

The chaos that follows a 'ta-da' moment is much more challenging than having navigated the change adequately from the beginning.

> **While resistance can seem unreasonable, irrational, and illogical, it is an innate human reaction to sudden change.**

CHOOSING DEATH OVER CHANGE

A 2007 study by Alan Deutchman, an American journalist, professor and author, demonstrated that people are more likely to choose death over change. When asked to change their lifestyle, including diet and exercise, only one in nine people made the change. Even after being told these changes could prolong their life, restore their health, reverse their diabetes, decrease their blood pressure and prevent worsening of their heart disease [5]. Eighty-eight per cent of people chose the path to death rather than make a change that would potentially prolong their life.

One person who is a true expert on death is Elizabeth Kübler-Ross, a Swiss-American psychiatrist and a pioneer in near-death studies. In her book, 'On Death and Dying', she discusses her theory of the five stages of grief, later known as the Kübler-Ross curve [6].

In describing the five stages of grief, Kübler-Ross uncovered the following pattern of adjustment:
  1. Denial
  2. Anger
  3. Depression
  4. Bargaining
  5. Acceptance

What Kübler-Ross discovered, through her interviews with dying patients and their relatives, was the essence of what humans experience during imposed change.

For this reason, the Kübler-Ross curve was later adapted into the Change Curve.

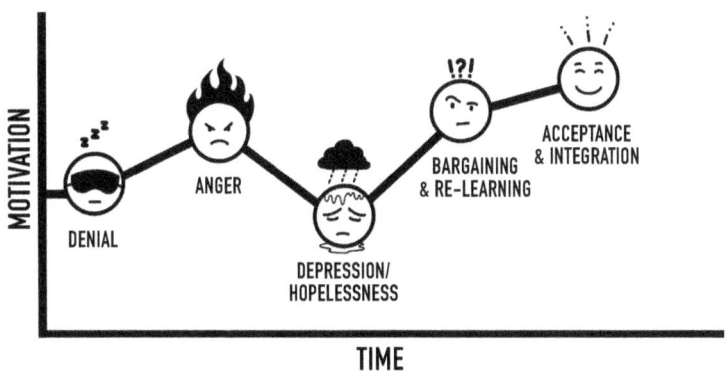

Figure 1.3 The Change Curve- an adaptation of the Kubler-Ross Five Stages of Grief [6].

The X-axis captures time, while the Y-axis represents motivation.

In relation to motivation, it is interesting that during the 'anger' phase, intense emotion can motivate people to perform, however, this spike in performance may be directed towards destructive rather than productive outcomes.

It's also important to note that each person will go through the change curve in their own time. Some may remain in the denial phase for an extended period or become angry and leave an organisation. Some may stay in the hopelessness phase to the extent that it affects their mental health and well-being. On the other hand, some may go directly from the announcement of a change to bargaining and relearning, swiftly followed by acceptance and integration.

How people go through the change curve depends on (a) how they are supported through the change journey and (b) a complex set of personal factors- both of which we will discuss in the following chapters.

In the meantime, let's revisit Nancy's story and observe her progression through the change curve.

Initially, Nancy was in denial about the changes to her role. This was apparent in her belief that management was bluffing and her refusal to leave the clinic for a newly assigned position. Subsequently, she remained in the anger phase for quite some time. Angry that a less experienced newcomer was replacing her, she sought to 'punish' the leadership team by cancelling patient appointments. She was so angry that she took down her accreditation certificates from the wall, leaving empty frames as a powerful message.

All parties were frustrated and stuck at a junction with no way forward. Leadership did not want Nancy to go due to her experience and rapport with patients. The newcomer was excited about her role yet needed guidance and mentoring that Nancy was unwilling to provide. Nancy's new team manager was also frustrated as they needed her as soon as possible.

I started by facilitating a discussion - the aim was to provide a forum where everyone could raise their frustrations and concerns, followed by further 'digging' to understand the underlying issues collectively. To no one's surprise, there were tears and profanities. I then made it clear that I was not the bearer of solutions; they were the ones who held the answers.

This was their clinic; they knew their roles, capabilities and patient needs. Ultimately, they needed to come up with a plan. It wasn't until I had mentioned the patients that the tension started to subside. Even Nancy's tightly clenched arms began to release. We were making progress towards acceptance and moving on from the destructive anger. Leadership had acknowledged how their communication of the changes to Nancy was ineffective. On reflection, they admitted they should have asked her opinion and supported her in using a computer before deciding to move her on. In return, Nancy acknowledged that she had overreacted and that her behaviour was unprofessional.

Reluctant to see her hard work left behind, they agreed to a mentoring and training program where Nancy would dedicate one day a week to teaching those new to the clinic. Nancy felt empowered to share her knowledge and expertise. At the same time, the newcomer felt she could bring new ideas to enhance the clinic. It was a mutually beneficial scenario. Nancy dedicated the other four days to working in her new area and learning from her new manager (moving to the 'relearning' phase). She was excited to discover she would interact with different patients, and it wasn't long before she finally entered the acceptance and integration phase.

Humans often respond to change as they respond to death, paralleling the grieving process.

KEY TAKEAWAYS

- When change is suddenly thrust upon us, our survival instinct is to fight, flee or freeze.

- 'Ta-da' moments instigate our human responses to resist sudden change.

- It is normal to go through different stages of change, including denial, anger, depression/hopelessness, bargaining/relearning and integration. However, how long it takes to go through these stages depends on how we navigate change.

ADDITIONAL RESOURCES

Scan the QR code at the end of the book to access articles and watch videos on why humans resist and battle change.

CHANGE CHAOS 02

> *Chaos is inherent in all compounded things.*
>
> Buddha

IT TAKES A PLAGUE

In the last chapter, we uncovered how our brain's survival instincts resist sudden change. Now we'll find out what happens at a global level when change is thrust upon us.

The sudden outbreak of Coronavirus (COVID-19) in 2020 was the most significant global change many of us have experienced. The normalcy of going to the shops, park, work or school changed in what seemed like an instant.

What did people do when they thought their survival was in jeopardy? What did organisations and world leaders do? Initially, the 'fight' response was prominent. People were fighting the requirement to wear a mask, measures taken to avoid the spread of the virus, vaccination mandates, and even fighting over toilet paper in the supermarket. The levels ranged from mild complaining to street protests that were quite counterintuitive to the fact that we needed to practice social distancing.

Others froze, preferring to believe they would not be affected, that it was not actually happening or that it was all some type of hoax. Then some chose to flee, shutting themselves and their families away at home and not allowing anyone to enter or leave. They were paranoid about everything and everyone, disinfected incessantly and thought any tickle in their throat was COVID-19.

When the hysteria died down and people started becoming more familiar with terms such as 'lockdown' and 'social distancing', new norms began to form. What was once foreign became a regular practice. Across the world, there was a necessity for things to change. Leaders changed regulations as often as they changed their outfits. I remember waiting for the weekly update from the Government to see what we could and couldn't do.

There was an apparent emulation of the Change Curve. Some people stayed in denial, breaking the rules they thought were unreasonable and continuing as if nothing was happening. Some were angry - at the government, retailers and even their family and friends.

Others entered a state of hopelessness and depression, especially when isolated with no support or someone to help them through the challenging times. However, many eventually progressed to relearning and integrating into this new way of living.

A poem published at the height of the pandemic highlighted that we were all 'in the same storm, but not in the same boat'. Our respective 'boats' represent each person's different journey due to our unique circumstances and experiences. Some people had an all-inclusive yacht, while others were frantically bailing water out of their broken-down dinghy.

However, it wasn't all bad. Many made the most of additional time at home with their families. I started this book, and we did some much-needed home renovations, which helped create a more pleasant environment. The kids started getting into more complex indoor activities such as Lego. We established a family tradition of Friday pizza and movie night and even started talking to our overseas friends more often.

Regardless of people's means, attitudes or behaviours, eventually, everyone had to adapt in some way - necessity indeed became the mother of invention.

A prominent example of the necessity to change was in healthcare. For decades, researchers have highlighted the effectiveness of implementing innovations such as telehealth. Research indicated that telehealth would allow practitioners to work from home, reduce the pressure on primary practice and emergency departments and improve self-management of chronic conditions, yet the adoption rate was very low.

A study into the barriers to implementing telehealth in regional Australia indicated that practitioners didn't want to utilise it because there was a preference for traditional ways of providing medical services. They perceived telehealth as time-consuming and lacked trust in the technologies [7]. It was rarely a priority for GPs, specialists or patients to utilise. This was a typical case of why change it if it's not broken.

However, when patients were prohibited from visiting clinics during the height of restrictions, there was no other choice- telehealth was very quickly adopted. Suddenly the barriers had dissipated. Consulting firm McKinsey & Company released a report stating that only 11% of consumers said they were interested in telehealth in 2019, compared to 76% post the outbreak of COVID-19 [8].

Similarly, employees had requested flexible arrangements such as working from home for decades. Most organisations were unsupportive or used it sparingly. Again, research had previously highlighted the benefits of flexible work arrangements, such as improved stress-related biomarkers [9], reduced absenteeism, increased bottom line margins, increased motivation, lower turnover intentions and increased job satisfaction [10] - yet flexible arrangements were seldom utilised. It was another case of why try something new and uncharted if the old way seemed to be working. Yet when organisations had no choice due to lockdown restrictions, they rapidly adopted online collaboration platforms enabling most non-front line staff to work exclusively from home.

Interestingly, video conferencing made its debut way back in 1964 by AT&T. It evolved from personal video conferencing applications to room/group-based video conferencing introduced in the workplace in 2000 [11]. In 2001, organisational adoption of video conferencing products such as Zoom and Microsoft Teams was as low as 10% [12]. The change brought about by COVID-19 was so swift and impactful that for Zoom alone, the number of daily meeting participants increased from around ten million in December 2019 to two hundred million in March 2020 [13].

Necessity and urgency have clearly shown how we can rapidly adopt innovations and adapt to new norms. Yet, why do people still resist change?

> **People had avoided change like the plague, and it took a plague to make people change.**

THE PENDULUM OF CHAOS

What feelings does the word 'chaos' stir inside of you?

At a conference, I asked over a hundred Change Managers to submit their responses to that question (larger text signifies the words mentioned more frequently):

Figure 2.1 Responses by Change Managers to the interpretation of the word 'chaos'

It's clear that most group members did not positively associate with the word 'chaos'. Unsurprisingly, given that humans are innately inclined toward logic, linearity and rationality.

Chaos is defined as 'complete disorder and confusion', a sentiment I often hear to describe the state when change is implemented. Chaos occurs because we are generally introducing change into a non-linear dynamic system.

Non-linear dynamic systems include organisations, families and communities. In these 'systems', multiple internal and external forces lead to dynamic actions and reactions that are unpredictable and non-sequential. This unpredictability is deemed chaos.

Change = Alteration from the status quo + Uncertainty + Confusion (all three are ideal ingredients for chaos)

In 1898, a French mathematician, Jacques Hadamard, was the first to suggest that if a small change is made in the initial conditions of an otherwise stable system, then that system's long-term evolution is impossible to predict. This thinking paved the way for the development of the 'butterfly effect' by Edward Lorenz in 1963, which states that even small changes in a nonlinear system can result in large differences later on [14].

What does all this mean?

Imagine a pendulum with several hanging weights. If we lift one of the peripheral weights a short distance (i.e. introduce a small change), the impact will be minor and relatively controlled. If we lift that same weight higher (i.e. introduce a bigger change), the impact will be bigger and last longer (continuous swinging of all the weights for a prolonged period). Now imagine if several weights are lifted simultaneously at different heights (i.e. introduce multiple changes of different magnitudes at the same time). This action will cause what is referred to as a 'chaotic pendulum', which means that the more unpredictable and complex the changes that happen to a non-linear dynamic system, the more chaotic the reaction will be.

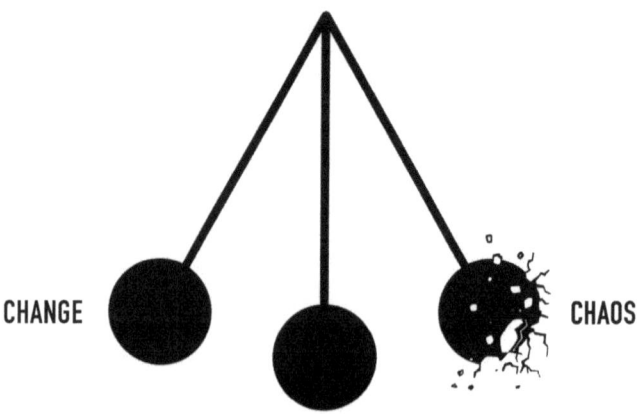

CHANGE   CHAOS

Organisations are very complex environments. Suppose an organisation has been functioning in the same pattern (the pendulum is moving in a regular and predictable motion). When several changes of various scales are introduced simultaneously, disrupting that pattern (multiple weights swung at different heights), the effect is unpredictable chaos (chaotic pendulum).

When I asked those same Change Managers how they would best describe the reality of the changes they have been involved in, most agreed it was simply 'chaos'. The truth is that nothing about implementing change happens in linearity or can be predicted. Why? Because humans are complex beings whose different responses to change are entirely unpredictable.

A 'rescue' project I was involved in for a government department was experiencing constant changes, causing unpredictable chaos. Most significantly, several ministerial changes occurred during the project. Changes in leadership at a government level often mean changes in priorities, systems and even the merging and separating of entire departments. By the time we came in, people were simply exhausted.

They had reached maximum capacity and showed high levels of change fatigue; they were overworked and still not seeing any results. Ultimately this led to a profound lack of trust.

In addition, the project exceeded its original scope, budget, and timeframe. This common experience has been a challenge for decades. A study undertaken in 2004, analysing fifty government projects over twenty years, found that projects involving technical innovation and systems development ran over budget by up to 200%. They also ran over the original contract duration by 54% [15]. The cost of project failure across the European Union alone in 2004 was €142 billion [16].

How did we 'rescue' the project? We didn't. We put an end to it.

The impact of the constantly changing 'pendulums' had to stop. The business needs had changed significantly since the original scope was defined, which meant that the proposed technical solution would not have been fit for purpose if we continued to push it through to fruition. Instead, we engaged end-users to clarify what was important to them while streamlining and automating processes causing bottlenecks and inefficiencies.

When we introduce change, the status quo is disrupted, inadvertently causing chaos. As different 'weights' at different 'heights' are added, the outcomes can be devastating. An essential part of navigating the chaos of change involves acknowledging and understanding this dynamic.

Chaos is inevitable during change, but those impacted suffer when we don't navigate it early.

THE COMPLEXITY OF HUMANS

From the stories about Adam and Nancy, it is evident that change can be difficult at any stage of life. However, why do some people have a higher tendency to embrace change whilst others actively avoid it?

To understand this, we must delve into the human psyche's complexity and the personal chaos that lives within us.

A model that helps us explore the complexities of humans is the Iceberg Model. The Iceberg Model was designed to help people discover the patterns of behaviours, supporting structures and mental models underpinning events.

In 1976, Edward Hall used this theory in relation to culture. In his book 'Beyond Culture', he describes that everything we do can be changed, however, once something is a learnt behaviour, pattern, or habit, it gradually becomes innate and, therefore, like the iceberg, sinks to the bottom and solidifies [17].

A complex network of factors contributes to our behaviours at an individual level. The Iceberg Model illustrates this underlying chaos. People only see the tip of the iceberg sitting above the water (behaviours) and miss what lies beneath the surface (experiences, values, beliefs etc.).

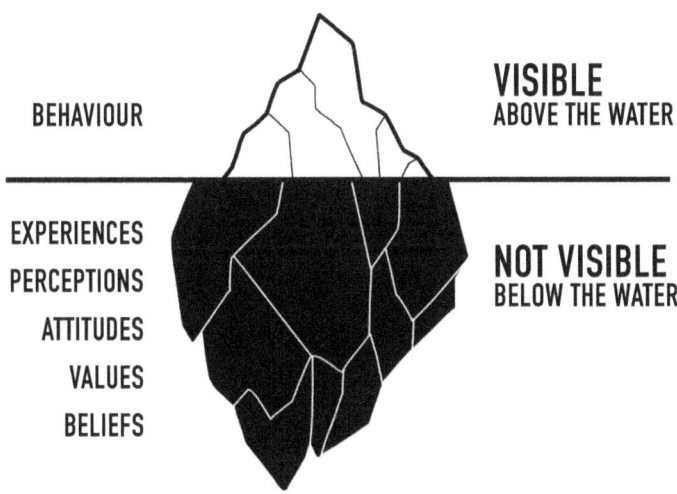

Figure 2.2 The complexity of humans showcased by Edward Hall's Iceberg Model of Culture [17].

Whilst we may appear similar as humans, underneath the 'surface', there is so much more to who we are. The challenge is understanding which factors below the tip of the iceberg are changeable (such as perceptions) versus deep-rooted beliefs that are much harder or impossible to change. It is also imperative to consider the things we ought not to change as they reflect who we are and what we stand for.

The Iceberg Model translates into an organisational setting when things learned, accepted and repeated consistently become part of how the organisation 'does things'. The change journey, therefore, requires unlearning, relearning, testing and rebuilding. 'Organisational culture tends to be unique, composed of objective and subjective dimensions. It is concerned with tradition and the nature of shared beliefs and expectations and is a powerful determinant of individual and group behaviour' [18]. It's essential to discern whether

proposed changes oppose or align with the culture.
If there is a lack of alignment, something has to give - either the proposed changes or the people whose values and beliefs are being challenged.

Adding to this complexity is whether someone feels a change will jeopardise their basic human needs being met.

At the start of my journey in change facilitation, I was involved in a program where we supported pharmacies to implement change and evaluate their progress.

In one pharmacy, the assistants agreed to identify ways to reduce the gifts sold in the store, so the space could be used to provide health services to patients. Upon my return three months later, it seemed as if the gifts section had expanded. When I asked the pharmacy assistants, they explained that the orders had already come in and couldn't be cancelled. However, I was certain there was an underlying reason, so I went digging.

After speaking to the pharmacy assistant in charge, I realised that she felt her job would be compromised if the gifts were gone. Her basic human need for security was jeopardised and manifested in resistance to change.

According to Abraham Maslow's Hierarchy of Needs [19], a sense of security is foundational, exceeded only by physiological needs. Therefore her actions were not surprising- she was simply preserving her livelihood.

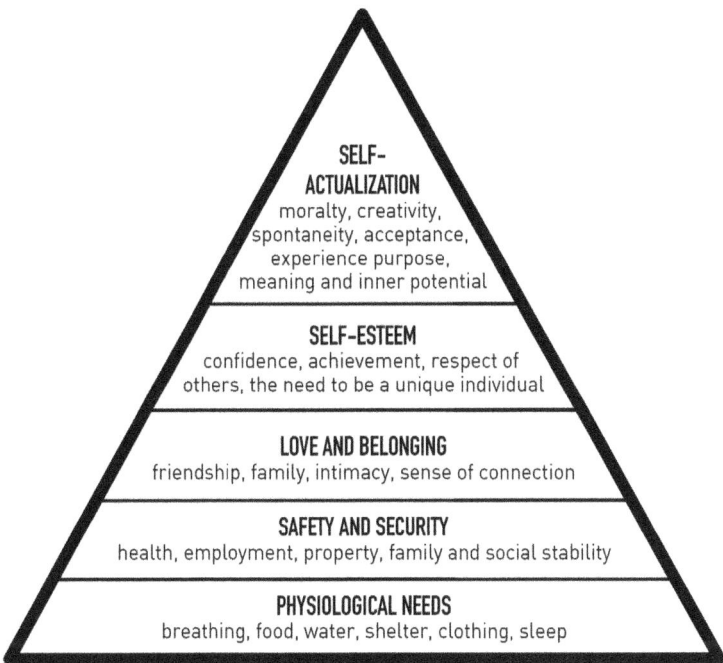

Figure 2.3. Basic human needs during change are showcased by Maslow's Hierarchy of Needs [19].

Upon making this discovery, I assured her that she would be trained to conduct the new health initiatives and that it was a matter of building capabilities in a different area and expanding her repertoire of skills rather than taking away her job. By the next visit, most of the gifts were gone.

When we spend time understanding the complexity of humans, we shift from focussing on surface 'negative' behaviour to the depth of what lies beneath.

KEY TAKEAWAYS

- At a societal and global level, external chaos can push us to fight, flee, freeze or adapt to our changing environment.

- When multiple changes are introduced at once without being adequately navigated, it can contribute to change fatigue, loss of morale and trust and inadequate use of time and money.

- Change resistance is related to our complexity as humans and can often be related to misaligned values and beliefs or when our sense of security is compromised.

ADDITIONAL RESOURCES

Scan the QR code at the end of the book to access articles and watch videos on the complexity of humans.

PART II
CHANGING CHANGE

TIME FOR A CHANGE IN
CHANGE 03

An old belief is like an old shoe. We so value its comfort that we fail to notice the hole in it.

Robert Brault

FROM LINEAR TO DYNAMIC

In the 1950s, Professor Kurt Lewin introduced the first organisational change model. Lewin was a German-American psychologist known as one of the modern pioneers of social, organisational and applied psychology in the United States. In one of Lewin's early writings, he developed a change model that states organisations first need to 'unfreeze' what they're currently doing, 'make changes' and then 'refreeze' [20]. Whilst this might seem simple, Lewin revolutionised organisational development thinking and triggered a movement that supported the notion that change can be positive.

Initially, I was critical of Lewin's theory for being overly simplistic and insufficient to cater for true change transformation. That was until I discovered that Lewin did not intend a three-step process but a dynamic change journey. The problem was that instead of viewing organisational change as complex and dynamic, researchers and practitioners continued proposing stepped models leading to what I term 'a lineage of linearity'.

Following Lewin, there were Lippitt's seven steps in 1959 [21], Kanter's ten change commandments in 1992 [22], Kotter's eight-step change model in 1995 [23], Nadler's twelve action steps in 1997 [24], Leucke's seven-steps in 2003 [25] and Hiatt's five-step ADKAR® model in 2006 [26].

Whilst some concepts in these models contributed significant value to the field of organisational change, I was curious to understand how they were applied in practice.

The following captures the experiences of people I spoke to regarding existing change practices:

"Change management is a bad word around here, we've been through fourteen Change Managers in the last two years, and every single one has failed. We're kind of scarred." - Head of Transformation at a Tertiary Education Institution.

"I have never come across a good change management approach... hold on (thinking)... nope. Every single time there has been a new person, who is overwhelmed and is so consumed by ticking boxes, but hasn't provided any real benefit to the project." - Project Management Consultant in Financial Services.

"I have seen a lot of top-down approaches to change, but never any granular bottom-up approaches that have truly brought people onto the change journey." - Head of Risk at a Tertiary Education Institution.

"Oh, the Change Manager- yes, they're the person who sits a bit far and always comes around asking us to fill in spreadsheets. We don't interact with them much beyond that." - Agile Coach in a Consulting Firm.

The feedback was consistent - people suffered from what I refer to as 'Post Change Stress Disorder' or 'PCSD' due to linear change management approaches.

I raised this at the conference attended by Change Managers (mentioned in chapter two) and was expecting to receive backlash, however, most attendees ultimately agreed.

Researchers have also highlighted that over the last fifty years, organisational change management has not fundamentally developed anything completely new [27], with many models being too linear and prescriptive in nature [28]. This poses a significant challenge due to the models' lack of flexibility to deal with the vast assortment of problems and issues that may be experienced during change [29]. In addition, such linear models have been deemed by researchers and change practitioners as too simplistic for implementing large-scale or complex changes [30].

Another classic example of a linear approach is the traditional schooling system. Most mass systems of education evolved from the 18th-century application during Industrialism. They followed algorithms and principles of standardisation and factory life [31] and have not significantly changed. In a video curated and narrated by Sir Ken Robinson titled 'Changing Education Paradigms', a powerful illustration shows children on a conveyor belt being 'produced' in batches as per their ages. Robinson observes that the only commonality among children seems to be their age and that they are batched according to their 'date of manufacture' [32].

The Program for International Student Assessment (PISA) measures fifteen-year-old students' reading, mathematics, and science literacy every three years. In 2018, the highest reading performance was for girls from Finland, the highest mathematics performance was for boys from Japan, and the highest science performance was for girls from Finland [33]. What was Finland doing differently to achieve these results?

Finnish schools utilise a dynamic and flexible approach, tailored and individualised to cater to each student's needs.

One could argue that this flexible and diverse approach to learning must cost an exorbitant amount of money. The truth, however, is that Finland does not spend as much money on education as other countries with less impressive PISA outcomes. In fact, out of all the countries assessed, Finland's spending was 15th for Primary School expenditure and 20th for Secondary School expenditure [34]. A more individualised approach costs less while achieving superior outcomes.

Similarly, organisational leaders assume that a dynamic and tailored approach to change is costly. On the contrary, using a traditional linear change approach is likely to cost more due to several factors:

- Additional time and money are spent to ensure people adopt the change.
- Effort is expended trying to follow 'best practice' rather than asking 'what is best for our practice?'
- Staff turnover increases due to eroded trust and 'post-change stress disorder', which costs more in the employment and induction process.

What is the key difference between traditional linear models and a dynamic change approach? Similar to the Finnish education system, it's a flexible, dynamic approach that allows for adaptable navigation and customisation according to individual needs - an approach we will delve into further in the next chapter.

Since the 1950s, there has been a lineage of linearity in change models. Whilst some concepts are sound, the models are unsuitable for dealing with the complexities and chaos of the modern change landscape.

FROM DIVIDE TO COMBINE

Combining the diagnosis and prescription

Imagine going to a doctor who spends the entire consultation diagnosing you, and once complete, they just send you home without your prescription- this would be completely unhelpful. On the other hand, imagine having a doctor prescribe you the same medication every consultation without undertaking any diagnosis- this would be completely unethical. Unfortunately, change models tend to be either solely diagnostic or prescriptive.

- **Diagnostic models** focus on diagnosing areas that should be considered during change. Two examples include Leavitt's Diamond, which highlights the structure, technology, people and tasks, and the McKinsey 7S model, which recognises structures, systems, style, staff, skills, strategy and shared values [35]. Whilst these models help explore where challenges such as misalignment may occur during change, they do not provide guidance on establishing potential solutions.

- **Prescriptive models** provide generalised solutions through a series of steps, irrespective of the challenges. These include Kotter's eight-step model [23] and Hiatt's five-step ADKAR® model [26], whose prescriptive nature is less accommodating to understanding the context and tailoring the strategies accordingly.

Ideally, we need a navigation system that ensures we consider and utilise both diagnostic and prescriptive approaches during change.

Combining implementation and adoption

During change projects, there is often a divide between:

- **Project implementation** is measured by a project's adherence to time, budget and scope.
- **Change adoption** is the level of engagement with the change being introduced and usage levels.

This separation potentially manifests into:

- Prioritisation of project implementation success over people adoption.
- Involving change teams halfway through, or worse still, at the end of a project rather than from its inception.
- Defining a project's success exclusively through implementation measures with people's adoption as an afterthought or completely neglected.

Researchers in project management have stated that a 'significant contributor to project failures is overlooking the impact of social/ psychological components (the people aspect)–significant components of the change phenomenon' [36]. In other words, project implementation must go hand-in-hand with people-focused adoption [37].

People will be an afterthought if a project is solely led and defined by scope, budget, and timeframes. Project implementation and people adoption must be intertwined in the DNA of any change from the very beginning. When we separate them, everything unravels.

Fortunately, I have met and worked with a project manager who understands and appreciates this critical intertwining of implementation and adoption during change. James Bawtree, co-author of 'The Strategy Implementation Gap', highly values and prioritises the change adoption aspect within a project. While working together, we observed that when implementation (scope, timeframe and budget) is prioritised over adoption (people), projects are doomed to fail, and those impacted suffer throughout the project.

When speaking to teams in these situations, they never feel in the driver's seat but are constantly dragged from one mandated time frame to another. The following word cloud captures the sentiment of teams I've worked with who have been on projects driven solely by timeframe and budget:

Figure 3.1 A word cloud depicting frustrations following a failed 'traditional' change project

One person I spoke to said, "I've had nightmares from this project, I haven't been able to take a holiday in three years, and I don't think I can keep going"- a clear sign of PCSD (Post Change Stress Disorder).

Co-designing change

Research has shown a positive correlation between high user involvement and project success [37]. When those impacted are not at the centre of change design from the beginning, drastic modifications may be required at a later stage with significant unavoidable costs [38].

I have observed this in multiple technology projects, where a small group of people (sometimes one person) gives specifications to the technology developers, and a platform or software is developed according to these specifications. The developers return months (or even years) later with a 'ta-da' moment, however, users quickly recognise that it is not what they need, leading to low adoption or re-starting the project from scratch.

Not only does this require additional funding, but it also significantly reduces the morale, engagement and trust of those involved.

When we constantly put those impacted at the centre of designing the change, it bridges their diverse involvement with the expertise to bring it to life. Such collaboration and participation in the design of a change increases its adoption and sustainability.

This 'co-design' approach is referred to as Human Centered Design (HCD), which has been used in multiple disciplines over the last few decades, including space engineering in NASA [39], medication adherence [40], consumer product design [41] and tourism [42].

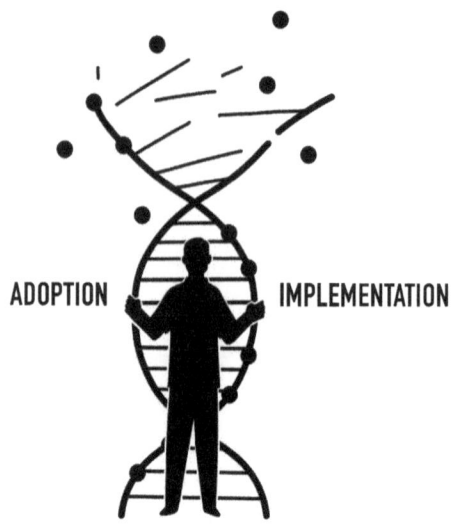

During a project with a university, we utilised the HCD approach by bringing together Deans of Faculty, academics, professional and administrative staff, and students to co-design an ethical leadership program. Using this co-design approach, we aligned all these stakeholders toward a set of shared priorities. As a result, they could create feasible solutions and take ownership of their specific roles and responsibilities to implement and sustain their proposed changes. This approach does take upfront time, effort, intentionality and meticulous planning. Yet, research shows that using HCD reduces development costs and increases user activities [43], addressing implementation and adoption measures.

Combining diagnostic and prescriptive approaches whilst intertwining implementation and adoption (with people at the centre) allows for more holistic change navigation.

FROM MANAGING TO FACILITATING

There are three main issues with the concept of 'managing' change:

Problem 1: The Change 'Manager' title

When our daughter Elaria was two years old, one of our friends made the mistake of greeting her with, "Hi Ellie". In a very serious tone, she looked them dead in the eye and responded, "My name is not Ellie, it's Elaria!" She has always loved her name and refused to be known by any other.

Just as names are central to a person's identity, the title by which we are known in the workplace plays an essential part in how we are perceived and navigate our role.

The Change 'Manager' title sets an expectation that they can 'manage' the people aspect of change. A manager is 'a person responsible for controlling, or administering an organisation or group of staff' [44].

The challenge, however, is that when it comes to change, we can't 'control' the reaction to it. If someone feels angry about a change, we can't just tell them to stop being angry. We also cannot 'control' how motivated they are about the change.

Therefore, the title 'Manager' sets Change Managers up to fail as change adoption is not a task that can be ticked off, controlled or managed.

Problem 2: Change Managers as 'doers'

For years, we strained our backs leaning over to tie Elaria's shoelaces for her, and if we were not around when they frequently became undone, she would trip over and hurt herself. Out of nowhere, one day, she offered to do it herself. It took a bit of patience and persistence, but within a week, she had mastered it. Instead of constantly being the 'doers' (painful for her and us), we simply passed on the skills and knowledge she needed to do it herself.

Unfortunately, Change Managers tend to be the 'doers' of change for the organisation, taking sole responsibility for communication, engagement, upskilling and bringing people on board. Upon moving on to their next project, they leave in their wake employees who have little understanding of how to maintain momentum and ensure the change is sustained in the long run.

Ron Ashkenas, an internationally recognised speaker, organisational transformation consultant, and co-author of the 'Boundaryless Organization', wrote a Harvard Business Review article in 2013 titled 'Change management needs to change'. In his article, he mentions that one of the problems facing the change industry is a lack of accountability for effective change management within the organisation [45].

Many organisations have adopted the view that, to some extent, 'risk' is everyone's responsibility (not just those with 'risk' in their title) to protect the organisation and its customers. I firmly believe that this same principle must apply to change. Change should be everyone's responsibility, not just those who have 'change' in their title.

Some organisations also revert to recruiting contractors or consultants to 'do the change'. This approach can disempower employees as they perceive that they are not trusted to own the change or adequately upskilled to navigate it.

Problem 3: Insufficient internal change capabilities

In his article, Ashkenas also writes that the managerial capacity to implement change has been 'woefully underdeveloped' [45]. In many organisations I have come across, people leaders (usually mid-level management) are rarely equipped with strategies to navigate change and deal with resistance.

Mid-level management is often stuck between a rock (senior leadership) and a hard place (their team members). Leaders push them to meet strategic objectives while their teams push for ease in their day-to-day operations.

In addition, such managers are often promoted due to their technical expertise and tenure rather than people and leadership capabilities. Therefore, it is no surprise that studies show that the highest resistance levels often come from mid-level management [46].

For these reasons, middle management must be equipped with the necessary skills to understand the science behind change resistance and how to navigate the chaos of change, ensuring they can effectively lead their teams through any change journey.

How do we address these challenges?

Whilst visiting Verona (Italy), Andrew and I seized the opportunity to attend a concert held in a first-century colosseum - right within the birthplace of opera.

As we listened intently to the majestic sounds that echoed in the open air, it didn't bother us that we couldn't understand the words because the beauty of the music transcended language barriers. I could not help but focus my gaze on the conductor. His use of hand gestures, body language and eye contact was fascinating. It was an artistic dance founded on a learned and universally understood language. He navigated a large group of musicians through the melodies, each bringing something unique to the performance yet working harmoniously together. It struck me that the conductor was a 'facilitator' who enabled the unity and collaboration of all these amazingly talented individuals.

The alternative to 'managing' or 'controlling' change is to 'facilitate' it.

The Change Facilitator's role is to unearth and leverage the team's diversity, considering that each person brings unique skills and experience. As the Change Facilitator navigates everyone toward the same destination, the team work in unison towards a harmonious 'change melody' and collectively builds on each other's insights.

Implementation research defines change facilitation as 'a technique whereby facilitators provide support to help individuals and groups realise what they need to change and how to make changes.' [47]

In healthcare, change facilitation has become a key component in supporting teams during implementing change in practice [48]. It has proven effective across various settings [49], such as nursing, general practice, and pharmacy.

The concept of shifting from change 'manager' to change 'facilitator' has also been examined extensively and shown to be an effective approach to building adaptable and cohesive teams [50].

Through change facilitation, the focus turns to leveraging and building the capabilities of people leaders and their teams so they are better equipped to navigate change. Rather than trying to 'sell' a change or encouraging people to 'buy in' to a change, which is often perceived as transactional, facilitation involves a united and collaborative change journey.

Like an orchestra conductor, a Change Facilitator brings different 'musicians' together to create a harmonious change 'melody'.

KEY TAKEAWAYS

- To navigate the complexity of people and chaos of change, we need to shift from prescriptive, overly simplistic linear change models to a more dynamic and tailored approach.

- A holistic 'diagnostic and prescriptive' approach is critical to finding the problem and tailoring the solution during change.

- Project implementation and people adoption must be intertwined in the DNA of any change from the very beginning.

- Change 'Management' gives the illusion that change can be controlled by those with 'change' in their title. However, a more facilitative approach is needed to unite people and leverage existing capabilities throughout the change.

ADDITIONAL RESOURCES

Scan the QR code at the end of the book to access articles, watch videos and listen to podcasts about the need to change the way we do change.

A TRANSFORMATION JOURNEY 04

> *A physician is obligated to consider more than a diseased organ, more even than the whole man - he must view the man in his world.*
>
> Harvey Cushing

THE MESSY CUPBOARD OF CHANGE

Andrew and I have always thought of ourselves as 'minimalists'. We don't like clutter, and everything we own has a purpose. When moving house, we thought it would be a breeze until we opened all our cupboards and looked under the beds. This was an opportunity to clean the old before moving into the new.

Luckily, I find organising therapeutic and satisfying. I love transforming physical spaces into something aesthetically pleasing and practical. I was excited about the possibilities yet couldn't help but feel a sense of anxious anticipation.

First, I needed to unleash the chaos by removing all the contents of the kitchen cupboard. It was a mess of doubled-up spices, packets of half-opened pasta, expired goods and questionable snacks. Until then, I had been living with the mess, rummaging to find what I was looking for, only to realise it had expired. Whilst I could simply take out the contents and dump them in the new cupboard, this was the perfect opportunity to refresh and innovate in my new space.

In any transformation or change, whether at home or work, unleashing the chaos will inevitably expose things that may have previously gone unnoticed, such as:

- Old mindsets
- Legacy systems
- Toxic behaviours

- Hidden agendas
- Competing priorities
- Inefficient processes
- Ineffective communications
- Inadequate experience

On the other hand, throughout that chaos, we might also find:

- Hidden talents
- Creative thinking
- New values
- Alternative technologies
- Innovative approaches
- New evidence-based strategies
- Outside of the box thinking
- More efficient systems and processes

Once I had everything laid out and could see the sheer amount of items, my motivation plummeted. It was much easier to distract myself with other things than to tackle the behemoth task of sorting through the chaos that was embarrassingly visible on my dining table.

Similarly, people may be excited at the beginning of an organisational transformation until they see the amount of chaos unleashed, causing their motivation to plummet. This is often referred to as 'the implementation dip', which is a dip in performance and confidence when a person comes across an innovation that needs new skills and understandings [51]. However, this dip is the critical tipping point in any transformation - teams or individuals may revert to their initial state, squeezing everything back as it was in the old cupboard and trying to live with it, or move forward to embrace and navigate the chaos.

Figure 4.1 The messy cupboard of change- intentionally unleashing the chaos

When I finally decided to tackle the task at hand, it was time to design how I wanted my new cupboard to look. I had undertaken some research beforehand and captured images of the 'ideal' cupboards posted on social media, however, each was for a unique need and space. Whilst it was all great inspiration, I needed to create something appropriate for our family and space.

Unfortunately, many organisations do not realise this soon enough. They seek to emulate competitors, follow 'best practice' or blindly adopt the latest innovation fads without considering their people and customers' unique needs. Often when this happens, the new shiny initiative or tool becomes another failed project collecting virtual dust. 'Shiny object syndrome is a human affliction, and it's all too easy to be lured into it' [52].

An effective strategy to avoid 'shiny object syndrome' and tailor the 'end product' to suit the needs of my 'end-users' (the family), was to involve them in the design of the cupboard. We started with a structured system to sort through all the items. There were separate piles for expired items, things we needed to pour into labelled containers and items which would go on shelves and turntables. Gradually, this systematic approach helped progress the chaos into order.

In an organisation, getting your people involved in the early stages of sorting through the chaos makes them more invested in the change and its longevity. They will also feel appreciated as a valued member and acknowledge that their thoughts and ideas are critical for the success of the change.

I also realised some essential tools and resources were missing that would enable our cupboard transformation, and therefore needed to make a few trips to our local homeware store to buy the organisational knick-knacks.

Similarly, teams may discover that additional tools are required to enable progress during organisational transformations. It may be a digital platform to enhance efficiencies, a new policy to tighten governance or an improved layout to improve collaboration. The key is to acknowledge a need to pivot and act upon it.

As we were bringing the new cupboard to life, it was essential to work on the most challenging part - adoption. The cupboard would be beautifully sustained if it were solely up to me. However, the reality is that I don't live alone and so we all had to test the new layout, ensure it was practical for everyone and agree on how it would be maintained. I asked my daughter if she could reach all the items to make her breakfast, but she couldn't, so we moved those items down a shelf. I checked with my son if he could reach the sweets and biscuits, and he could, so we moved them higher. Finally, I asked Andrew to find different items to ensure the layout was intuitive, and we re-arranged it according to his feedback. This was crucial because Andrew is the better cook and will be the cupboard's biggest user.

Testing, monitoring and feedback are critical in every organisational transformation. We need to adopt an iterative approach (covered in a later chapter) to ensure we iron out what needs to be adapted to suit our ongoing and often evolving needs. My preference is usually for a 'go-live it period' rather than a 'go-live date' as it provides an opportunity to understand what is working and what needs to be adjusted.

Sadly, people often walk past the 'old cupboard' oblivious to the problems within it or choosing to ignore the 'expired items' and 'questionable smells'. They accept that they spend an inordinate time finding the needed items and may complain about it consistently. However, taking everything out and unleashing the chaos can seem far too overwhelming - it often seems easier to deal with inefficiencies and broken systems. However, it is more productive to proactively, intentionally and collaboratively unleash the chaos.

Unleashing the chaos is the trigger for unleashing hidden talents, opportunities and true transformation.

NO SILVER BULLET

A system is defined as a 'regularly interacting or interdependent group of items forming a unified whole' [53]. 'Systems Thinking' was coined by Barry Richmond in 1987 and can be described as the ability to; think abstractly to, accommodate different perspectives, solve a problem with unclear scope, understand and cater to diverse contexts, make sense of complex behaviours, identify dependencies and stakeholder relationships, and attempt to predict changes to that system [54].

American systems scientist Peter Senge explains systems thinking as a framework for seeing interrelationships and patterns of change rather than static snapshots [55,56].

In other words, systems thinking involves a deep understanding of a dynamic setting (such as an organisation) and the potential impacts when introducing change. The relevance of 'systems thinking' is how we view and navigate change in its entirety.

My research included a two-year implementation study involving six Change Facilitators (myself included) supporting nineteen pharmacies across Australia. The objective was to enable pharmacists to implement transformational changes in their practices by providing patients with health services such as diabetes care and medication management. These services were predominantly government-funded, which meant a greater financial return for the pharmacies.

Over the years, many independent pharmacies have struggled to compete (particularly on price) with larger chains, as their business models were not built on low margins. This scenario was a typical case of business survival being reliant on change.

The Change Facilitators visited the pharmacies once per quarter. They recorded all their observations and interactions, including exploring change barriers, the strategies we established to overcome them and evaluating the change progress based on the effectiveness of these strategies. As this information formed the foundation of my PhD, I was thankful for the vast amount of data collected during the implementation study, but there was so much to consume that I may as well have been eating data for breakfast.

Our analysis uncovered 36 barriers to change and 120 change strategies [57]. There was no clear barrier or 'silver bullet' strategy in implementing change.

With our 'systems thinking' hats on, it was essential to consider the interplay of barriers and strategies, however, limited research had been conducted in this area, so we were entering uncharted waters.

In interpreting the data, simple statistical analysis was insufficient. For example, if a strategy was only used once and was successful, it would return a 100% 'resolution rate' compared to another strategy used ten times and working for nine, resulting in a 90% resolution rate. Without knowing how often a strategy was conducted, the automatic assumption would be that the strategy with a 100% resolution rate was more effective.

To overcome this, we leveraged the Advanced Analytics Institute at the University of Technology Sydney (UTS), who used a 'machine learning' approach known as 'decision trees' to extrapolate the results and accurately predict how effectively a change strategy would overcome a particular change barrier. Using this process, we could reach almost 97% data accuracy in predicting a change strategy's effectiveness when addressing a specific change barrier.

For example, to overcome the change barrier of 'a lack of knowledge and experience', the strategy with the highest predicted effectiveness was to 'create a collaborative environment conducive to change' (99.8%), followed by 'equipping stakeholders with training' (93.4%). Surprisingly, training was not the most effective strategy for building knowledge and experience during change.

To overcome the implementation barrier of 'a lack of individual alignment with the change', the strategy with the highest predicted effectiveness was to 'ensure stakeholders contribute to the change' (98.79%), followed by 'empower stakeholders to develop objectives and solve problems' (83.13%), and then to 'create a case for change' (82.86%).

This finding opposes models such as ADKAR®, which state that the first thing we should do is raise awareness of the change (or create a case for change). Instead, contribution towards the change was more effective than raising awareness.

Now that we had predictive, quantitative data that linked barriers with tailored strategies, the next step was to identify strategies with the highest predicted effectiveness that overcame the most barriers - that's when we started to see patterns in the data.

To validate or dismiss the patterns, we used the same approach (explore barriers, establish strategies and evaluate progress) during a Randomised Controlled Trial (RCT), but with different change facilitators, pharmacies and interventions implemented.

Across both studies, the patterns were consistent - providing us with a consistent set of principles that would form a dynamic framework to navigate the chaos of change.

There is no one clear strategy or barrier in change. We need to explore all the barriers, establish the right strategies and evaluate progress.

A DYNAMIC CHANGE FRAMEWORK

After four years of research, several published studies, a 50,000-word thesis and various real-world applications of our approach, we built a framework to help organisations, researchers, practitioners and even families navigate the chaos of change.

Why a framework?

Think back to the days before a GPS navigator or Google Maps. What did we use? For many of us, we started our driving experience using the dreaded Street Directory book. At the young age of seventeen, when I could finally drive on my own, the thought of going to a new place made me slightly anxious. It was even worse if there were roadworks, at which point I would usually end up on the phone with my father, asking for directions.

The Street Directory was a linear and static form of navigation. We now have dynamic and live navigation systems to help us adapt and change course where and when needed. Such navigation systems enable us to quickly evaluate our position and recalculate our route, so that we arrive at our desired destination faster and with less anxiety (ultimately improving our journey).

A framework is defined in the Cambridge dictionary as 'a system of rules, ideas, or beliefs used to plan or decide something'. What we needed was a 'system' to navigate change, one that provides the flexibility to start at any point within dynamic and guiding parameters. This system is the '6E Change Facilitation Framework.'

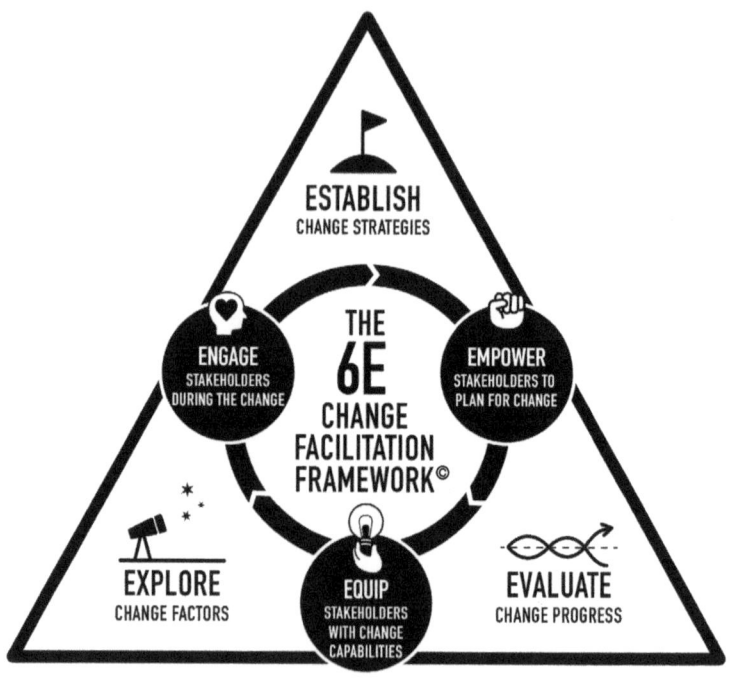

Figure 4.2 The 6E Change Facilitation Framework by Dr Lydia Moussa [58].

Shaping our framework

Two particular shapes help to reflect both an iterative and dynamic approach to change. For this reason, they are used in our 6E Change Facilitation Framework.

Shape 1: *The Circle*

The circle emphasises the importance of iteration and the need to continuously re-assess aspects that must be addressed throughout the change journey. In this case, it acknowledges that transformation is never ending if we want to evolve and thrive, rather than just survive, in VUCA environments.

Shape 2: *The Triangle (Delta)*

A shape often neglected in change literature is the uppercase delta (Δ) - ironic as it is often used as the mathematical and scientific representation of change. The triangle represents the dynamic nature of the framework. We can leverage each 'corner' according to what is required at that point in the change journey.

From steps to principles

A 'principle' is defined as 'a fundamental proposition that serves as the foundation for a system of belief or behaviour or a chain of reasoning' [59]. The 6E Change Facilitation Framework sets out six guiding, evidence-based principles (rather than prescriptive steps). These principles enable Change Facilitators to implement and adopt change successfully. Principles also allow for more dynamic movement according to the needs of the stakeholders and implementation progress. This dynamic approach is deemed a more realistic depiction of the activities conducted by Change Facilitators in practice, as all parts of the organisation do not necessarily move in unison [29,60].

Combining Implementation and Adoption

Another concept we wanted to capture within this framework was the intertwining of implementation and adoption. As highlighted in the previous chapter, the separation of 'project' from 'people' hinders collaboration, causes competition for priorities and eventually leads to a breakdown of trust. The 6E Change Facilitation Framework, therefore, combines:

Innovation Implementation principles (the outer triangle), which:

- Explore Change Factors
- Establish Change Strategies
- Evaluate Change Progress

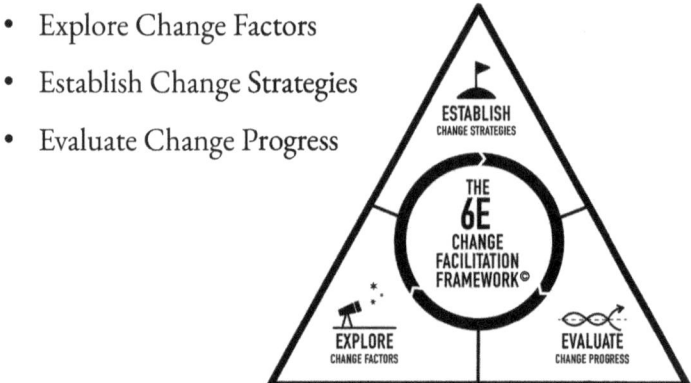

Stakeholder Adoption principles (the inner circle), which:

- Engage stakeholders during the change
- Empower stakeholders to plan for change
- Equip stakeholders with change capabilities

Where to start?

In a linear model, knowing where to start is easy- it is the first step. In a dynamic framework, however, the best place to start is where you are in the change journey.

Option 1: *Start by understanding the problem using the 'Explore' principle.*

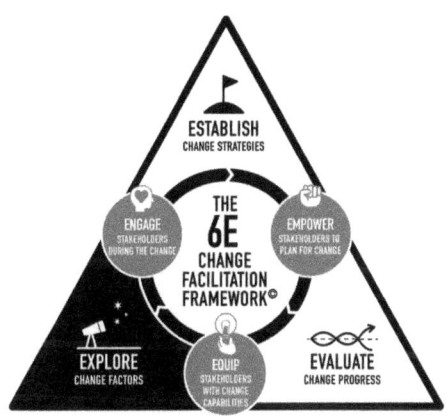

Perhaps an organisation doesn't yet understand any issues they need to address for the change to be successful (i.e. the 'diagnosis'). In this case, they must explore their current change factors.

Option 2: *Start by addressing the known problems using the 'Establish' principle.*

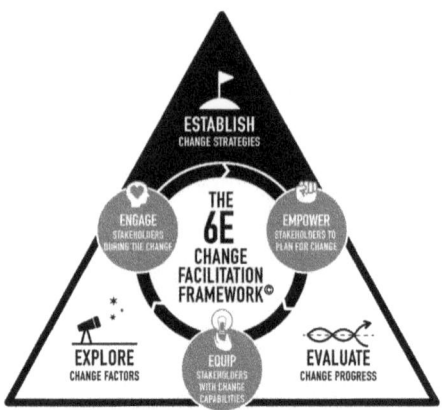

If an organisation already understands issues that need to be addressed, they need to establish (i.e. 'prescribe') suitable strategies. For example, if a lack of clarity around objectives is the barrier, they can establish strategies to clarify and align change objectives.

Option 3: *Start by assessing the impact of a problem or the progress of a strategy using the 'Evaluate' principle.*

Alternatively, an organisation may want to define the extent of a problem, hence, they would evaluate relevant baseline measures before any strategies are implemented. Or perhaps, the organisation may have already implemented a strategy and would like to evaluate its effectiveness.

Essentially, we need to tailor the starting point according to the needs of the organisation and the people impacted by the change.

People at the centre and heart of change

The 6E Change Facilitation Framework ensures that during every implementation principle, we are constantly putting people at the centre. When we put people at the centre of:

- Exploring change factors - they can be open with what is working for them and what isn't.
- Establishing strategies - they can solve their challenges.
- Evaluating change progress - they take ownership of monitoring and measuring their performance.

In the following sections of this book, we will delve into each of these principles, including their impact, practical application and contribution to successful change.

> **We developed a dynamic change framework that combines implementation with adoption, using guiding principles to facilitate human-centred transformation.**

KEY TAKEAWAYS

- For change to be successful, we need to unleash and embrace the chaos that comes with it.
- There is no one size fits all strategy for change; we need a dynamic approach in the form of a framework.
- The 6E Change Facilitation Framework allows us to dynamically navigate the chaos of change, wherever we are along the journey, as we:
  - Explore change factors.
  - Establish change strategies.
  - Evaluate change progress.

  While ensuring we continuously:
  - Engage stakeholders during change.
  - Empower stakeholders to plan for change.
  - Equip stakeholders with change capabilities.

ADDITIONAL RESOURCES

Scan the QR code at the end of the book to access published research on the 6E Change Facilitation Framework.

PART III

3E's
FOR IMPLEMENTATION

EXPLORE 05
CHANGE FACTORS

> *Not everything that is faced can be changed, but nothing can be changed until it is faced.*
>
> James Baldwin

FACTORS FAR AND WIDE

Andrew and I love to visit wineries. When we speak to winemakers, it's incredible how small environmental changes can affect the entire harvest for that year. There are some changes they can predict from year to year, but others come totally by surprise and could ruin an entire harvest in a single hour. One winemaker told us it had been nearly six years since their last great harvest, with reasons ranging from hailstorms to bushfires, floods, birds and insects. In addition, an array of standard metrics must be consistently measured to produce a wine bottle worthy of the shelves. If this is what it takes for one bottle of wine, imagine the number of complex factors we need to address when unique humans are involved during change.

Change factors

As mentioned in the previous chapter, during our research, we uncovered 36 factors in one setting that prevented successful change [57]. We refer to these as 'change factors'.

ADAPTABILITY

COMMUNICATION

CULTURE

MINDSET

NEEDS

POLICIES

SUPPORT

TIME

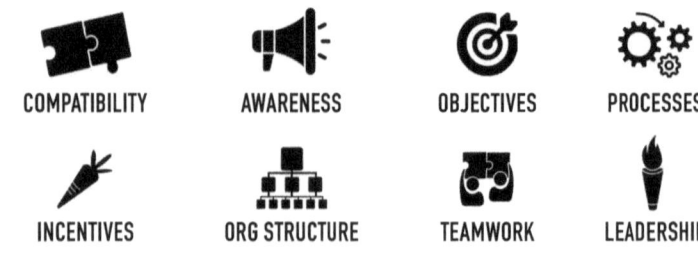

Figure 5.1 Examples of change factors that can act as enabler or prevent change success

Whilst this is a comprehensive list, these change factors were only what we identified during our research - many others could exist in different settings and project implementations.

Also, it is important to note that change factors can act as barriers or enablers to successful change [61].

For example, when stakeholders within the organisation have the 'skills' required to enable change, then 'skills' becomes an enabler for successful change. If there is a lack of skills related to an upcoming change, 'skills' becomes a barrier that needs to be addressed.

Figure 5.2 Example of 'skills' acting as a change barrier or enabler

'Leadership' is one of the most critical change factors - if leadership engagement and endorsement of the change are present, it becomes an enabler for change. If, however, there is a lack of leadership engagement and endorsement, this becomes a significant barrier to successful change implementation.

The factor I am always asked about is 'self-efficacy'. Self-efficacy influences how people feel, think, behave and motivate themselves [62]. During change, if a person has low self-efficacy, they have low confidence in themselves to implement the change. Low self-efficacy often stems from underlying factors such as a lack of knowledge and experience about the change, lack of resources to aid in the change and lack of capacity to deal with the change.

What makes the *'Explore'* principle in the 6E Change Facilitation Framework different from other diagnostic models, is that instead of leveraging a set of pre-defined factors, people are encouraged to explore all possible factors unique to their change, specific needs and particular settings. Therefore utilisation of the *'Explore'* principle in different organisations will often yield change factors unique to that particular setting.

Even within an organisation, factors discovered across different teams can vary significantly. One team's most prominent barrier may be 'processes', whilst for another, it may be 'culture'. It is, therefore, imperative to work at a granular level with teams to overcome change barriers specific to their needs.

It's also possible that a change factor may act as a barrier for one team or person but as an enabler for another. Or a change factor may be a barrier in one situation and an enabler in another similar instance. For example, a study exploring the barriers and enablers for migrant women entrepreneurs showed that culture could act as both a barrier and an enabler [63]. Cultural characteristics such as thrift, hard work and reliance on family labour can facilitate entrepreneurship [64,65], whilst cultural norms, expectations and religious beliefs can act as barriers [66].

With a potential multitude of factors in a given project, how do we categorise or make sense of them? The below diagram is an adapted representation of the Consolidated Framework of Implementation Research (CFIR) [61] - it displays change factors at different levels of an organisation's ecosystem.

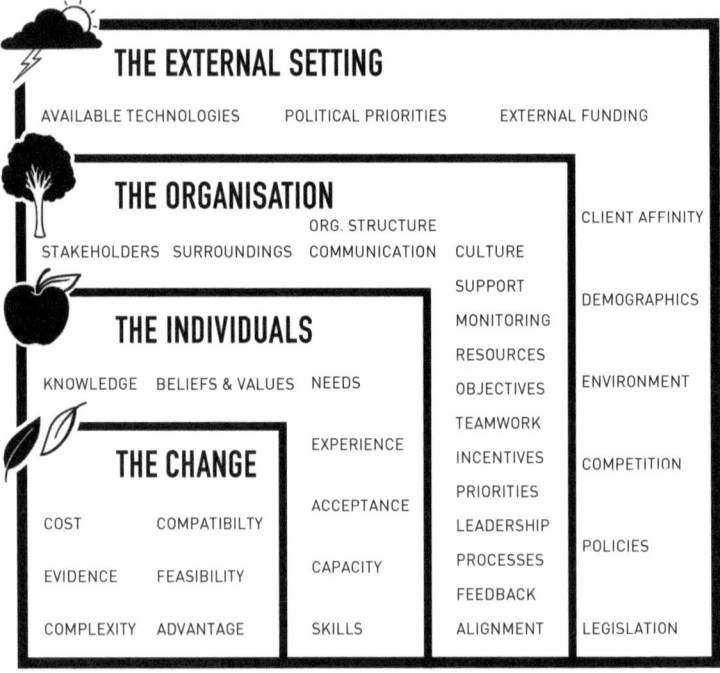

Figure 5.3 Change factors across different domains
- an adaptation of the CFIR Framework [61].

Using an example of implementing new software in an organisation:

The change - (also referred to as the intervention) factors at this level can include; the cost of the software, evidence of its effectiveness, advantages of its application in this particular organisation, how adaptable or tailorable it is, and its complexity.

The individuals - factors at this level relate to individuals within the organisation, including; their knowledge, skills and experience regarding the change, individual self-efficacy, capacities for the change, personal alignment with the change, specific needs and individual priorities concerning the change.

The organisation - (also referred to as the inner setting) factors at this level relate to the organisational setting. For example, is the software easily accessible? Are there experts to assist with the implementation, training and ongoing support? Have processes and policies been updated? Is leadership role-modelling the use of the new software? Does the IT infrastructure allow for such software? What about the internal culture- is it conducive to such innovations?

The external setting - I also like to call the external setting the 'out-of-our-control setting'. It can often be the catalyst for change if we are forced by external circumstances such as competitor pressure, changes in policy or legislation, a health crisis, funding challenges and changing regulations.

The 'change' and 'outer settings' constantly apply pressure onto the individuals and the organisation. If this pressure is too much, the individual and organisation suffer.

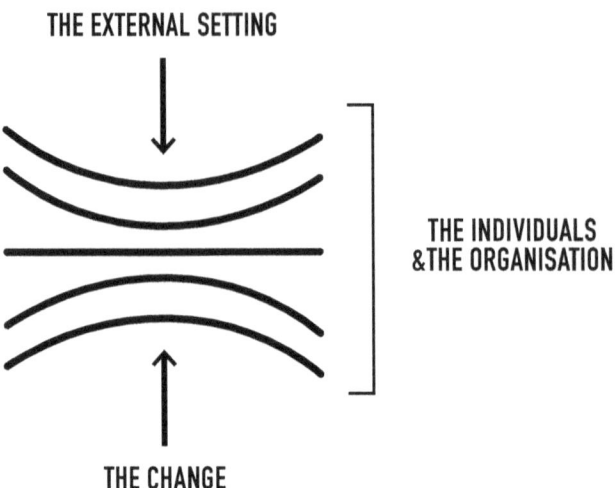

Figure 5.4 External and change pressure on the individuals and organisation

For this reason, exploring and addressing change factors across the different levels is critical to creating adaptable and resilient individuals and organisations.

Many factors can enable or prevent change success – we need to explore and understand them to navigate the chaos of change.

REBELLION, RUBBISH AND RAMIFICATIONS

In 2015, I was asked to help a community group understand what was causing unhealthy family environments. Parents shared that their teenagers were disengaged, with some turning to pornography, cyberbullying, drugs and alcohol. I commenced my engagement by facilitating several focus groups with representatives across parents, teenagers, teachers and community leaders.

At first, everyone other than the teenagers focused on 'quick fix' strategies such as internet filters and removing 'bad' associations. In the debate over 'quick fixes' compared to more sustainable solutions, I encouraged everyone to explore the underlying factors rather than surface symptoms.

We asked, "what do teenagers seek more than anything else?" As we delved deeper and ensured that teenagers were involved in the discussion, some real deep truths emerged.

The teenagers shared that they were often spoken 'at' rather than spoken 'with'. They avoided going home as they felt misunderstood and even dismissed, seeking instead to be around people who would accept them the way they are. Teenagers simply wanted someone who could talk with them and a place where they felt an unconditional sense of belonging.

When we started to shift the conversation towards this sense of belonging, the parents in the room started to reflect more inwardly - beyond blaming social media, computer games and peer pressure. They began to question what they were doing (or not doing), resulting in this sense of detachment. Following some intrinsic reflection and deep discussions, the parents highlighted a lack of:

Alignment - between husband and wife, causing a divide within the family.

Knowledge - of how to bring up teenagers, with parents often defaulting to the parenting techniques they experienced growing up, which was usually misaligned with the current needs of their children.

Communication - was the prevailing barrier. Usually, it was easier to speak 'at' their child without explaining everything. Seeking their children's opinions seemed unnatural as they didn't experience this growing up.

Time - as parents were too busy to provide one-on-one attention to their children and dig deeper to understand their needs.

Once the parents took ownership and accountability for their teenagers' lack of belonging and defiance, they could address the right underlying challenges.

The need for parent ownership is highlighted in a study where teenagers (aged thirteen to seventeen) and their parents were surveyed in 3,000 U.S. households, along with 267 face-to-face interviews. The study findings [67] encourage us to 'stop defining adolescence as a social problem and adolescents as alien creatures, strange and menacing beings, perhaps even monsters driven by raging hormones, visiting us from another planet'. Most teen problems are linked to adult problems - as such, adults need to 'get over their fear of young people' and start engaging them to solve problems together.

In another community project, I was asked to help find solutions to their waste problem. With thousands of people attending various gatherings over the week, the amount of waste produced, and in some cases not disposed of correctly, was becoming overwhelming. They had tried multiple strategies to control the rubbish situation in the past, including:

- Placing signs to raise awareness of the need to keep the grounds clean.
- Creating a video awareness campaign of the problem and sharing it on social media channels.
- Sending announcements via email to the members.
- Purchasing additional bins, including for recycling.
- Organising 'clean-up' days once a quarter.

Despite this, the community still had an enormous amount of rubbish, and the ramifications included excessive time, money and effort to manage it. They found that a strategy may work for a few weeks, but things would return to how they were. Excitement about the video faded, the hard work from the clean-up day was abolished the following week, and realistically speaking, not many paid attention to the email announcements.

As we spoke to more people, peered into rubbish bins, and observed behaviours, it became clear that this problem stemmed beyond the volume of waste.

The factors we uncovered included:

- **Needs and priorities** - food providers needed to use items such as cardboard pizza boxes, which quickly filled up the recycling bins and overflowed into regular bins.

- **Workflow and processes** - there were many bins, however, they were dispersed throughout the grounds rather than strategically placed next to each other, making it difficult for people to separate food from recyclables.

- **Mindset and behaviour** - adults didn't dispose of their rubbish before leaving their tables, which meant children followed this behaviour. There was an expectation that someone else would clean the rubbish leading to a lack of ownership and accountability among members.

- **Alignment and teamwork** - volunteers would be the only ones tidying up the grounds, rather than embedding these behaviours into all members, therefore, such behaviours became a norm.

- **Knowledge and education** - to our surprise, many people were unclear on the recycling rules, and without appropriate education, how could we expect them to change their mindset or behaviours?

In a study on waste management, a range of similar barriers was highlighted, including culture, lack of education, competing priorities and lack of incentive [68].

By using a 'systems thinking' approach (i.e. looking at the entire ecosystem where the change needs to happen and exploring all the change factors that were acting as barriers to change), we realised the rubbish was a symptom of much more profound, interrelated factors. We could now systematically implement tailored strategies to address each factor, working together to own and solve the problem. One example was a 'collect and earn' system - they educated their members on using bespoke recycle bins for cans and bottles, from which the community could actually 'earn' money from their rubbish.

Figure 5.5 A whole system view of factors contributing to waste management

The key is to examine the entire system, determine all the factors contributing to the problem, and tailor our change approach to address these.

GLOBAL AND CULTURAL FACTORS

Whether navigating change at a local or global level, the *'Explore'* principle of the 6E Change Facilitation Framework is critical in determining the factors that can enable or prevent successful change.

Having worked with several global organisations, I have found that regardless of the organisation's size, there is always a way to explore and uncover change factors.

During one global transformation project, we asked country leads to explore and identify their change factors.

We found the following top five common barriers:
1. Resources
2. Mindset
3. Training
4. Self-efficacy
5. Feedback

The following table contains reasons they identified for experiencing these barriers:

Change Barrier	Explanation of change barrier	Region	Possible reasons highlighted
Resources	People are not well equipped with tools that enable change to succeed	Africa, Asia, Europe, North & South America	• Capability • Budgets • Lack of well-defined plan • Lack of coordination • Competing priorities • Limited change resources • Not tailored to local needs • Complex systems that are not user-friendly • Unclear responsibilities
Mindset	People's mindset negatively affects the implementation of the changes	Africa, Asia, Europe, North & South America	• Lack of willingness to change • Level of comfort with status quo • Uncertainty of what success looks like • Fear of change • Silo mentality • Short-term focus
Training	People are not equipped with the right capabilities to enable the planned changes	Europe, North & South America	• Lack of time • People's low motivations • Changes in roles • Lack of budget
Self-efficacy	People are not confident in their own capabilities regarding the change	North & South America, Asia, and Africa	• Lack of information or vision • Lack of clear roles and responsibilities • Duplication of tasks
Feedback	People are not told about the progress of change implementation and adoption	Europe, North & South America	• Lack of process for feedback and review • Fear of negative feedback • Lack of clear communication • Lack of time for feedback • Lack of openness and transparency around feedback

Figure 5.6 Top change barriers during a global transformation project

One of the barriers which appeared across every region was 'mindset'. A negative mindset towards the change may be due to various reasons, however, in this project, the strongest sentiment was an unwillingness to change. This prompted me to ponder whether some regions and cultures are naturally more resistant to change. One person who has dedicated his research to this is Professor Greet Hofstede, founder of 'Culture Dimensions' [69]. Hofstede outlines several dimensions to assess cultures, one of which is the 'Uncertainty Avoidance Index'.

The Uncertainty Avoidance Index (UAI) depicts a society's tolerance for uncertainty and ambiguity. It indicates to what extent a culture makes its members feel uncomfortable or comfortable in unstructured situations [69].

In a 1980 study undertaken by Hofstede, 116,000 questionnaires were sent to participants across fifty countries to understand which countries were more likely to resist change versus those more accepting [70].

Some have argued that this research is somewhat outdated. Conversely, others have indicated that culture has been instilled throughout centuries and, therefore unlikely to have changed in a few decades.

Nevertheless, this research helps us to appreciate differences in the affinity for change across cultures and be more conscious of how to navigate it.

According to the study, the following countries showcased the highest and lowest UAI Scores.

Countries with the highest avoidance of change	Greece (highest), Portugal, Guatemala, Uruguay, Belgium, El Salvador, Poland, Japan, Peru, Argentina
Countries with the lowest avoidance of change	Singapore (lowest), Jamaica, Denmark, Sweden, Hong Kong, United Kingdom, Ireland, Malaysia, India, China

Figure 5.7 Countries exhibiting the highest and lowest Uncertainty Avoidance Index [70].

This confirmed findings in our project, whereby countries such as the United Kingdom and China were well on their way to adopting the changes, whilst countries such as Japan and Argentina had more difficulty.

Having this understanding helped to effectively address the barrier at a local level through additional coaching and facilitation support. For example, in addressing a negative mindset towards the change, one country lead created a focus group to explore the challenges perceived by the end users and asked them for ideas towards navigating those challenges (they were now actively involved in defining solutions).

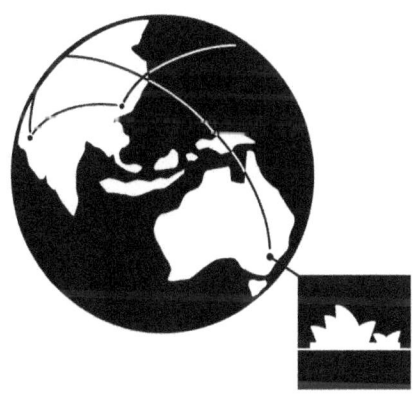

During large-scale changes at a global level, we cannot underestimate the importance of understanding barriers and tailoring strategies to meet the needs of local settings. When we neglect to do so, we risk local teams simply continuing as they were and avoiding making the changes for as long as undetectably possible. This can mean years of delay in implementation. However, if we support implementation at a local level from the beginning, change becomes more efficiently and effectively implemented and adopted.

Exploring change factors at all levels with all people can ensure we unearth and navigate any challenges in change - wherever they lie.

KEY TAKEAWAYS

- The *'Explore'* principle allows us to take time during our change journey to determine which factors hinder (barriers) and promote (enablers) change success.

- To give the right medicine, we must make the correct diagnosis. In the same way, we need to explore and identify the correct change barriers to tailor an appropriate change strategy.

- We need to look at the entire ecosystem where the change is occurring to discover all the factors contributing to the problem we are trying to solve.

- Even at a global scale, we need to explore the overarching change factors and drill down to the local level to explore and understand the granular factors that may enable or prevent successful change.

ADDITIONAL RESOURCES

Scan the QR code at the end of the book to access a 'Change Factor Diagnostic' that you can complete with your team, family or organisation.

ESTABLISH 06
CHANGE STRATEGIES

> *Rowing harder doesn't help if the boat is headed in the wrong direction.*
>
> Kenichi Ohmae

PAIN-KILLER OR ANTIBIOTIC?

I had a tooth that was always giving me trouble, and the pain would randomly flare up for years. Each time I would simply mask my symptoms with painkillers rather than visit the dentist to check what the issue was. On one occasion, the pain was unbearable. Thankfully, my brother-in-law is a dentist, and he booked me in for an immediate x-ray. After analysing the results, he relayed that the tooth was infected beyond repair and the only solution was to remove it.

Had I gone to the trouble of taking an x-ray as soon as the symptoms arose, a set of antibiotics would have saved my tooth. I had opted for a short-term painkiller solution rather than understanding my pain's underlying cause and implementing a long-term solution.

The old saying, 'prevention is better than cure', doesn't just relate to our health, but every aspect of our lives. It is much more worthwhile to dig deep upfront to uncover the underlying cause of a problem than to mask it with 'painkiller' solutions.

What better case study to understand the impact of 'painkiller' solutions than the opioid epidemic that crippled the United States from 1999 to 2019. Two decades of painkiller abuse resulted in the death of over 700,000 people due to opioid overdose, including prescription and illicit opioids [71].

The short-term pain relief these powerful drugs offer puts the user and physicians in a conundrum. Do they leverage these potent compounds for the humane treatment of pain and suffering, or do they risk inflicting a different type of suffering through addiction? [72].

Physical pain can be unbearable and difficult to push through, but we can form somewhat of a parallel to change. Do we opt for 'quick fix' solutions that may provide short-term relief, a spike in excitement and an illusion of hope, or do we persist through the chaos in pursuing longer-term, sustainable and healthier solutions?

I've observed numerous fads being implemented by organisations to spike engagement and improve morale, culture and outcomes. There's the on-site barista to encourage people back into the office, table tennis to help people connect, or free food after hours, so people work later. These attempts are usually unsustainable, superficial and ineffective in creating long-term, intrinsic and transformational change.

Figure 6.1 Quick fix vs long-term solutions

Employee training could also be a 'quick fix' painkiller solution. When working with clients to build their internal change capabilities, I ensure they understand that one training workshop will not suddenly make them adaptable and resilient. People may be motivated by it in the short term, but this dissipates if it is not coupled with ongoing application and support.

Researchers and practitioners agree that training is not the only answer, particularly when implementing behavioural changes. Decades of research on workplace training suggests that training does not work [73], as often, a lack of knowledge is not the only factor uncovered during change. Therefore, we must address all the factors that arise to ensure we've provided targeted 'antibiotics' where needed.

As a former pharmacist, I love using medical analogies - from antibiotics to vaccines. In 2021, we began to see the light at the end of the terrible COVID-19 tunnel with the availability of vaccines. Countries that had been heavily affected by the pandemic eagerly bought it en-masse. By June 2021, six months after vaccinations became available worldwide, Australia had a 15% vaccination rate, compared to the United Kingdom at 59% and the United States at 52% [74].

At that point, COVID-19 cases in Australia were rare, hence the government had lifted many restrictions. COVID-19 seemed like a distant memory, and we were finally returning to some sense of normality.

That is until it all changed again.

COVID-19 cases spiked from almost zero to hundreds within a few days, prompting state governments to reinforce severe restrictions. The lack of planning meant that when vaccinations were finally made available, demand initially outstripped supply as people rushed to be vaccinated for their safety and to reach milestones that would remove restrictions.

During transformation, leadership often opt for short-term painkiller solutions that provide the delusion that things are going well. Then, when it is clear that things are not going well, leadership may react by mandating changes without adequate planning and resourcing. The outcome is that whilst teams may have the desire and will to make change happen, their hands are tied due to insufficient resources and support.

When establishing strategies during change, we must look for long-term 'antibiotic' solutions rather than quick-fix 'painkillers'.

GLOBAL VISIONS TO GRANULAR MEASURES

Humanity strives toward ambitious goals such as ending global poverty or addressing climate change, however, the challenge often seems insurmountable. Where would we even begin? The complexity in the implementation, adoption and navigation of such global actions seems unfathomable, not to mention the red tape and navigation of political agendas.

The United Nations (UN) laid out seventeen Sustainable Development Goals (SDGs), which were 'a universal call to action to end poverty, protect the planet and improve the lives and prospects of everyone, everywhere' [75]. All UN Member states adopted the seventeen goals in 2015 as part of the 2030 Agenda for Sustainable Development, which set out a fifteen-year plan to achieve the goals.

Underpinning each development goal (change goal) are targets (change objectives) and indicators (change measures) - all aligned to the overall change vision.

Using the first SDG as an example:

- Change vision - end poverty, protect the planet and improve the lives and prospects of everyone, everywhere.
- Change goal - end poverty in all its forms everywhere.

- Change objective - by 2030, eradicate extreme poverty for all people everywhere, currently measured as people living on less than $1.25 a day.
- Change measure - the proportion of the population living below the international poverty line by sex, age, employment status and geographical location.

When using any navigation system (in our case, The 6E Change Facilitation Framework), we insert our destination and choose our preferred route - this is the change strategy. The below components form the change strategy:

Change vision - an inspiring statement towards a common destination.

Change goals - a breakdown of the vision into overarching themes.

Change objectives - relevant, specific, measurable and timely targets.

Change measures - a qualitative/quantitative metric to evaluate objective progress.

The following chapters will delve into what makes an engaging change vision and the different types of change measures. In the meantime, allow me to illustrate this further using a hypothetical example of an organisation implementing new software.

- Change vision - be the leader in next-day delivery service.
- Change goal - reduce time spent in the dispatch process.
- Change objective - a 20% reduction in dispatch processing in three months.

- Change measure - the time to insert information into the software.

We can also establish these change strategies at home.

When Elaria was seven years old, her teachers mentioned that she had trouble finishing her work in class. Being a social butterfly, she loved a good chat which could often distract her from the task. We first asked if she wanted to improve, to which she replied, "of course." When prompted further about why she wanted to improve, her answer was, "so my teacher could be happy with me."

At this point, we knew her improvement was not yet intrinsically motivated, so we dug deeper to help her understand that it is not about what her teacher thinks - but about her personal development, growth and learning. Whilst she understood this, her valid concern was, "I don't see how my learning is improving". This can be true for many of us; when we get caught up in day-to-day work, rather than establish strategies that enable us to constantly measure our growth, we simply wait for our annual performance review.

We then asked Elaria what she would like to achieve (her change vision). Her response was to "enjoy learning in class", made possible by "improving my work", "finishing tasks by myself" and " feeling happy while doing my work" - three clear goals.

We broke down these goals into relevant objectives, from which we then created tangible change measures so that she could clearly follow her improvement and growth. Using one of the goals as an example:

- Change vision - a more enjoyable learning experience in class.
- Change goal - complete homework unassisted.
- Change objective - a 10% increase in unassisted work time in two weeks.
- Change measure - time to complete a task without asking for help.

Within two weeks, Elaria had increased her unassisted homework time by 10% and felt more confident seeing her progress. The aim was not to obtain a seemingly untenable mark or to rely on an external report. It was about actively and intentionally making incremental changes using clear objectives and measures, where she could self-evaluate and celebrate her growth.

I use this approach to help build organisational transformation strategies. This is through co-designing the change vision, ensuring alignment with the organisational vision and breaking the vision down into clear goals, relevant objectives and tangible measures, providing them with a systematic approach to navigate what can often seem like an insurmountable journey.

> **As we navigate change, we must be clear on where we aim to head- that's the change strategy, which includes; a compelling change vision, clear goals, relevant objectives and tangible measures that meet the needs of those impacted.**

WALLS VERSUS BOUNDARIES

"We don't talk about that in this family". That's the response most of my friends and I received growing up when we brought up any slightly taboo topics with our parents. Subsequently, this built walls between our parents and us. We couldn't be as forthcoming with them, making establishing strategies together very difficult.

The same applies in organisations when management avoids difficult conversations or creates change strategies in isolated board rooms without collaborating with those impacted. This creates walls in the organisation that turn into silos, resulting in increased resistance, division and lack of trust.

Walls are impermeable partitions between those in 'power' and those affected by their decisions. In a family where parents say things like "it's my way or the highway," children can feel hopeless and frustrated that their opinions and thoughts will not be heard or acknowledged. In an organisational setting, leaders can create walls by introducing change mandates or 'ta-da moments' without consultation or prior discussions with those most affected by the change.

Walls provide those in 'power' with a sense of control and shield from internal or external influences. Sometimes they are built with good intentions, for example, to 'protect' children from potential harm.

However, we often find that children have clever ways of 'climbing' over the wall without their parents' knowledge or safety net.

Similarly, those in power can intentionally or unintentionally build walls in an organisational setting with good intentions, for example, minimising consultation on a change so they don't 'waste people's time'. However, dissatisfied staff will fight, flee or freeze, and continue to do so until worse and often irreversible damage is caused.

Walls are also often built to demand respect. However, this 'forced' respect tends to stem from fear. In an organisational setting, this leads to a lack of employee engagement, trust and willingness to innovate [76].

During change, walls are a significant barrier to collaboration, ideation, unity and trust. Division and fear of speaking up lead to underlying resistance, which becomes more challenging to navigate as people do not feel they can openly discuss their concerns for fear of being reprimanded or shut down.

How do we break down walls whilst still having boundaries?

Rather than building fear-fueled, siloing and suffocating walls, boundaries help to align and guide people towards a common goal. They act as the dotted lines on the road through which we travel along our change journey.

In an organisation, values drive behaviour and change strategy [77,78]. A set of values helps unite individuals within an organisation under a shared ethos and agreed ways of working.

It is, therefore, not surprising that value-led companies outperform others in areas such as growth in revenue, rate of job creation, growth in stock prices and profit performance [79].

In addition to establishing a vision, goals, objectives, and measures, we also need to establish values; these help us decide how we will get to our destination (what actions are appropriate and which are not).

Who needs to come up with these values?

Everyone.

Parents may take the first step in a family environment to facilitate the discussion with all members - questions about what is realistic and acceptable need to be asked together with the expectations of reciprocity. If respect is a value, parents also need to respect their children through how they speak and behave towards them both in private and public.

In an organisation, leaders may need to take the first step towards desiring, facilitating and role-modelling the values. However, values need to be co-designed with those expected to live them, i.e. the entire organisation.

Furthermore, using values as boundaries and aligning these to an organisation's change strategy enables more effective navigation of change. For example, if 'learn and grow' is a value within the organisation, when testing innovative ideas during change, learning from failed attempts should be acceptable and even sought after for teams to grow.

Creating boundaries based on values also enables sustainable success despite leadership changes, particularly if they have been co-created with employees. They become the boundaries in which the entire organisation operates regardless of who comes and goes.

The impact of values on organisational change

Whilst working at BPAY Group, my husband Andrew realised the culture was very different from anywhere else he had been - specifically, that people truly 'lived' the values. My curiosity about their success led me to interview their CEO at the time, John Banfield. John indicated that upon commencing with BPAY Group, he wanted to take an inside-out, value-driven and facilitative approach to their transformation. As such, he initiated their journey by co-designing the values through the involvement of all employees.

As a leader, one of his first activities was to role model what it means to break down walls and establish values that provide boundaries for the cultural transformation they wanted to create. In the next chapter, I'll share the outcome of this values-based approach.

> **We prevent division and maintain respect by establishing value-based boundaries rather than building impermeable walls.**

KEY TAKEAWAYS

- The '*Establish*' principle allows us to tailor our change strategies according to the needs of a particular setting.

- We must avoid short-term' 'pain-killer' solutions that only target surface symptoms and establish systemic 'antibiotic' solutions that target the entire system and address the relevant barriers.

- When navigating change, the 6E Change Facilitation Framework operates as our navigation system, while a clear change strategy lets us know where we are heading. Components of a change strategy include an aligned change vision, clear goals, relevant objectives and tangible measures.

- Rather than building impermeable walls, we need clear value-based boundaries to guide behaviours and ways of working when navigating change in an organisation or family.

ADDITIONAL RESOURCES

Scan the QR code at the end of the book to access case studies on transformations across various industries.

EVALUATE 07
CHANGE PROGRESS

Measure what you value, instead of valuing only what you can measure.

Andy Hargreaves

WHY NOT BOTH?

In the previous chapter, I mentioned establishing change measures as part of a change strategy, but how do you measure change success?

Are you more inclined towards facts and figures (thinking with your head), or do you look for sentiment, stories and quotes (feeling with your heart)?

I vividly recall a television advertisement where two men argued whether soft-shell or hard-shell tacos were better. A little girl settles it with a shrug of her shoulders and a sweet voice as she asks, "Why not both?" An excellent question, indeed.

Researchers, practitioners and executives are known to display opposing views concerning measuring success - some prefer quantitative, whilst others qualitative analysis. Quantitative analysis includes statistics and scales, whilst qualitative analysis includes observations, verbatim comments and interview/focus group outputs.

In my research, I took the advice of the taco girl (and my supervisors, of course) and utilised both. I recorded the number of professional pharmacy services adopted (quantitative), barriers experienced by those in practice (qualitative), strategies used by facilitators (qualitative), and the number of times these strategies were effective in overcoming the barriers (quantitative). Using quantitative and qualitative measures is known as 'mixed method analysis' [48].

By combining what people say, feel, believe, hope and think with non-refutable facts and figures, we gain a more holistic picture of the change journey.

One particular 'quality of life' research showed the importance of combining qualitative and quantitative evaluations to better understand how people measured it [80]. One aspect of the research was to analyse the impact of the 'neighbourhood' on people's quality of life. Through interviews, researchers realised that people's definitions of 'neighbourhood' varied significantly. Therefore, a scale of how people rated their neighbourhood was irrelevant unless considered alongside the diverse interpretations.

One of my favourite case studies illustrating the power of combining quantitative and qualitative evaluation is the Lucky Iron Fish Enterprise (LIFE). LIFE is dedicated to fighting global iron deficiency [81]. According to the World

Health Organisation (WHO), iron deficiency affects two billion people and is prevalent in women and children across low-middle income countries. As iron supplements are fairly costly, there needed to be another solution.

When working in Cambodia in 2009, Dr Christopher Charles learnt that Cambodians had one of the highest rates of iron deficiency in the world, which led to physical and mental developmental difficulties. Charles set about visiting villages to promote the placement of a small iron ingot in their cooking pots that release iron directly into food. Whilst the research was sound, it was met with much scepticism and reluctance from the Cambodian people.

Therefore he spent more time with Cambodians, observing their lifestyles and rituals. This led him to redesign the ingot to resemble the Kantrop fish, symbolising luck and 'health-giving powers' in Cambodia. Shortly after, compliance rates for the ingot exceeded 85% - markedly higher than those for iron pills and micronutrient powders.

Using qualitative data through observations and discussions with locals, as well as quantitative measures for adoption, compliance, and hemoglobin levels, Lucky Iron Fish could improve the quality of many people's lives.

Measuring the intangible

What about measuring the intangible? Using qualitative and quantitative analysis to measure aspects such as culture can be particularly important, especially during periods of change.

> *"Culture eats strategy for breakfast, operations for lunch, and everything else for dinner."*
>
> Peter Drucker

A toxic culture and negative behaviours can significantly affect an organisation if left unchecked. But how can culture be checked?

One way to measure culture is to embed the organisation's values into employees' performance and goals. Regular evaluations of these values become central to performance conversations and expectations and eventually become embedded in organisational culture.

In the previous chapter, I mentioned my interview with former BPAY Group CEO John Banfield. As we chatted, behind us lay a beautiful mural to remind employees of the values they created together. I asked John, "What makes these values more than a pretty picture on the wall?" He responded that they were deeply embedded in the organisation's ways of working, within individual performance goals and part of all discussions around strategy, culture and growth.

The co-designed values became a measurable way to evaluate and monitor the progress of their culture. What was the outcome? In 2018 and 2019, BPAY Group was recognised as an AON Hewitt 'Best Employer' for building the type of culture that drives collaborative transformation. In 2020 and 2021, they were one of Australia's top five Best Places to Work by Great Place to Work®, one of the world's most comprehensive assessments of workplace culture.

More importantly, every employee I spoke to at BPAY Group, including my husband, loved the culture - a testament to a successful transformation.

> **Numbers might not lie, but they do not tell us the entire truth - we also need to hear what people say, feel and hope.**

E-VALUE-ATION

An important question to ask when implementing change is 'what added value will it bring, and how will this be evaluated?'

Organisations may find it easier to make assumptions on what success looks like based on similar competitor use cases, best practice recommendations or past experiences. However, what may work well for one organisation, team, or individual may not work the same for everyone else. Defining ongoing, measurable and validated evaluations that consider the 'value-add' to those directly impacted is essential.

The value in regularly evaluating a change is that it:
- provides insight into the effectiveness of the change within the desired setting.
- enables the discovery of continued improvements.
- gives an early view on whether to continue, re-evaluate or cease a change program.
- highlights valuable data on how the change positively or negatively affects those impacted.
- helps determine whether the approach can be replicated in other situations or needs to be tailored.
- ensures all voices are continuously heard throughout the change.
- provides different perspectives and highlights any extremities in the data.

Conversely, when we don't regularly evaluate change progress, it can lead to:

- spending excessive time, effort, resources and financial investment on an inappropriate change for that setting.
- a lack of positive changes to that setting.
- low adoption rates as people do not see the benefits or how the changes relate to them or improve their ways of working and output.
- increase in change fatigue and loss of motivation.
- loss of trust in the change, leadership and the organisation.

Two common metrics to evaluate change progress include time (efficiency) and quality (effectiveness).

Time (Efficiency)

> *"Time is what we want most, but what we use worst."*
>
> William Penn

In our research, a 'lack of time' was cited among 20% of the most common implementation barriers [57]. A lens through which we can better understand the time factor are metrics that measure efficiency - these include:

- Allocative efficiency - people getting what they need.
- Productive efficiency - minimum cost of input to produce maximum output.
- Technical efficiency - maximum output with the given input.
- Dynamic efficiency - involves improving both allocative and productive efficiency over time.

Rather than simply outlining "this change will save teams time", we can add more value by explaining what type of efficiency they will experience and to which part of their role. For example, the 2010 World Health Report [82] suggested that between 20% - 40% of all health resources might be lost to the various forms of inefficiency mentioned previously. Such findings led to many countries examining technical efficiencies across their hospitals [83–85].

Quality (Effectiveness)

While efficiencies are related to the optimum use of time and resources for maximum output, effectiveness is concerned with the organisation achieving its vision, mission and goals [86]. In the words of Peter Drucker, "efficiency is doing things right; effectiveness is doing the right things."

Research in the field of Implementation Science identifies effectiveness measures (often referred to as implementation outcomes) that can add significant value during change [87], including:

- **Acceptability** - involves capturing the perception among the staff of how agreeable or satisfied they are with the idea of the change (for example bringing in a new system).

- **Adoption** - includes the intent of uptake among those to whom the change is proposed and actual uptake. Measuring intent requires qualitative metrics to understand the reasons behind their position, however, post-implementation uptake is generally more quantifiable (for example, the number of users).

- **Appropriateness** - captures whether a change is relevant and compatible with the setting; in other words, is it a good fit? For example, if the entire organisation exclusively uses one type of software for all email, file sharing and video conferencing capabilities, it may not be appropriate for one department to implement an alternative solution.

- **Implementation costs** - these depend on several factors, including the cost of the change and its implementation in that setting. For example, implementing a new software may introduce regular license fees. Additional costs include the time and resources spent on training users to ensure successful adoption. These higher value costs are sometimes missed during the early stages of a project.

- **Feasibility** - considers aspects such as availability or funding to train users or infrastructure to support a new system and, subsequently, determines whether such aspects can be adjusted to implement the proposed change.
- **Fidelity** - is the extent to which a change was implemented as intended. For example, a new software implementation may be misused, or people may find more innovative ways to use it.
- **Adaptability** - is the degree to which a change can be tailored, refined or reinvented to meet unique needs. There is an inherent tension between fidelity (i.e. how strictly we adhere to the original use case) and the need to adapt (i.e. ensuring that the change is fit for purpose and solves a problem for the people impacted).
- **Integration** - measures how well the change is integrated into a setting. Has the system become integrated into the way the team works? This requires short to medium-term evaluation and monitoring, leading to the final implementation metric (sustainability).
- **Sustainability** - refers to the extent to which the change has become part of the organisation's day-to-day ways of working (i.e. how institutionalised it has become). This requires long-term evaluation and monitoring of adoption, utilisation and feedback from end-users.

The key is knowing what metric will add the most value during evaluation.

In one project, the organisation was replacing an IT system used by its internal staff. Interestingly, end users indicated that whilst using the new system added more time (reduction in productive efficiency), it significantly improved their data quality and reporting output, which was critical for audit and governance (increase in appropriateness measures).

There is no one-size-fits-all change metric - each team will value a different metric and we, therefore, have to tailor our evaluation measurements accordingly.

> **By placing value on what we evaluate, we can determine and measure what truly matters to different individuals and teams during change.**

PERFECTION VERSUS ITERATION

Whilst perfection is something many spend their entire lives seeking, it can often be an illusion that traps us in its seductive embrace, leaving us disappointed and broken.

> *"At its root, perfectionism isn't about a deep love of being meticulous. It's about fear. Fear of making a mistake. Fear of disappointing others. Fear of failure. Fear of success."*
>
> Michael Law

In 2018, a study was conducted to examine group generational differences in perfectionism [88]. The study looked at three types of perfectionism:

- Self-oriented perfectionism - irrational desire to be perfect.
- Socially prescribed perfectionism - perceiving excessive expectations from others.
- Other-oriented perfectionism - placing unrealistic standards on others.

The study found that between 1989 and 2006, the self-oriented perfectionism score increased by 10%, socially prescribed perfectionism by 13%, and other-oriented perfectionism by 16%.

The World Health Organisation states that due to the increasing rate of perfectionism, more young people hold irrational ideals for themselves, which is likely to blame for increasing rates of anxiety and depression [89].

Similarly, when organisations constantly aim for perfection, it affects their progress and employee well-being, leading to emotional exhaustion and burnout [90]. During the chaos of change, stifled progress can cause a cascade effect that delays communication, adoption, the realisation of change benefits and ultimately, the loss of trust in the change.

From perfection in silos to iterative progress together

Classic project management typically follows a 'waterfall' process of planning and execution, where expected results are communicated relatively clearly by the customer (internal or external) at the beginning of the project [91]. Whilst this provides stability and structure and is intended to deliver a 'perfect' end deliverable, it is very rigid, with minimal room for adaptations and iterations to cater for changing needs and environments. Once the customer has outlined their requirements, it can take months or even years to build, depending on the project's scope. At the end, the customer is presented a 'ta-da' moment, hoping that the result has met their expectations.

On the other hand, 'Agile' approaches do not focus on comprehensive, advanced planning and the linear, exact 'execution' of a plan [92,93] but rather on iterative, flexible approaches that quickly adapt according to changing customer needs [94].

Many organisations are recognising the need to adopt iterative approaches to project delivery, enabling them to adapt to rapidly changing customer demands and environmental circumstances typical in our VUCA world.

Some organisations find it challenging to adopt iterative methods, as they feel uncomfortable with the concept of a Minimum Viable Product (MVP). Having 'minimal' rather than perfect outcomes may be unpalatable for organisations that rely on stringent compliance. However, the longer the isolated design takes to reach perfection, the larger the potential disparity between customer expectations and product design.

Adopting an iterative approach, developing an MVP and maintaining constant collaboration enables early feedback. Customer needs can be better met through continuous improvement, rather than waiting for the unknown and unpredictable feedback at the end (after a significant amount of time and effort has been spent).

An added benefit to early and iterative evaluation and feedback is that we 'fail fast and early'. During one of our Agile training workshops, an attendee raised their concern about how this would affect a project, however, in my opinion, this was better than 'fail slow and late'.

We reduce the potential for a fight, flee or freeze response by involving users in continuous evaluation and feedback. Customers become part of the solution rather than simply highlighting the problems that need to be fixed, creating co-ownership of the change and increasing early adoption.

An iterative approach is commonly utilised in software design and implementation and is becoming widely adopted across other use cases. In one project, an all-encompassing visual mural was created to support the rollout of an organisation's values, vision and strategy. We showcased the first MVP to the executive team in black and white sketches. After initial discussions, feedback was provided from which the second MVP was designed - still in black and white but with more details. After further feedback from the executive team and representatives from the organisation, further changes were made, including the addition of vibrant colours. This process not only invited collaboration and constructive feedback but ensured everyone took ownership and had pride in the final product. When I asked the executive team how long this process would have taken in their previous 'waterfall' approach, they said possibly more than a year (compared to only one month using an iterative, agile approach).

The approach can even be helpful in our personal lives. Casting back to my cupboard transformation story in chapter four, I was conscious of consulting with my customers (the family) during each stage of the change. Their early evaluation and feedback helped identify what worked for them and what didn't. Had I alternatively created a 'ta-da' moment, they may have initially been wowed at how it looked, but over time, it would have inevitably raised usability issues.

Evaluate early and provide feedback on progress constantly because whether we fail or succeed, we consistently learn and move forward together.

KEY TAKEAWAYS

- The *'Evaluate'* principle is critical for monitoring and evaluating change progress, ensuring we are continuously on the right track, and alerting us when we go off-course.

- We need to consider both the qualitative and quantitative aspects of measuring change to provide a more holistic view of progress.

- There are many metrics to evaluate change progress; when choosing the right metrics, we need to ensure they add value to the change and those impacted by it.

- When considering the frequency of change evaluation, an 'agile' approach allows for constant iteration, improvement and end-user feedback - as opposed to the more traditional 'waterfall' approach that aims for perfection.

ADDITIONAL RESOURCES

Scan the QR code at the end of the book to access diagnostics for feedback and monitoring that can be used with your team or organisation.

PART IV

3E's
FOR ADOPTION

ENGAGE STAKEHOLDERS DURING THE CHANGE 08

 *Engaging is not informing; it is active two-way communication that seeks to understand and build trust.*

Dr Lydia Moussa

BUILDING AND BRIDGING THE VISION

Every time I saw the Sydney Harbour Bridge, I couldn't help but admire its grandeur and ponder how such an amazing structure was built. The researcher in me had to find out, and it gave me an even more profound appreciation of this iconic landmark.

Since the 1800s, city planners had been looking for ways to replace the cross-harbour ferries with a bridge. In 1911, John JC Bradfield was appointed to make this happen, but it wasn't until after the Sydney Harbour Bridge Act passed, that construction finally commenced in 1925.

Bradfield's vision was for the bridge to be more than just a road across the harbour. He was advocating for a design that would; unite communities (linking south to north Sydney), boost the economy (following the Great Depression), and future-proof the city (for population growth) [95].

His vision never wavered, even though it took eight years to construct. It was a mammoth undertaking and represented international advances in bridge technology in the early twentieth century. Over 2,000 workers were employed in various aspects of its building, including engineers, architects, blacksmiths, stonemasons and painters. Nothing of this scale had ever been attempted in Australia, and the work involved was often difficult and extremely dangerous.

Bradfield instilled a vision so powerful that it would inspire an entire city. Many workers risked their lives to build this engineering masterpiece (some of whom died during construction), and over eight hundred buildings were destroyed to make way for this single structure.

A compelling change vision will describe the change's existence and what it strives to accomplish [96]. The vision should aim to be; brief, clear, future-oriented, stable, challenging, abstract, desirable, and able to inspire [97]. In addition, while a change vision can focus on the output of the organisation, it is more successful when it takes into consideration the industry, customer or the unique competitive advantage and innovation it provides [98,99].

When there is no common change vision, priorities will sway depending on; external pressures, differing team priorities, changing leadership (including their characters and agendas), and negative employee behaviours. Conversely, when people feel that the vision is clear and aligned from the beginning and throughout the change journey, there is a higher correlation to effective outcomes, job satisfaction and lower employee turnover rates [100].

Co-designing the change vision

Unlike Bradfield, however, change visions in current times cannot be created in isolation or by the leader- no matter how inspiring the leader may be. The change vision needs to be co-designed with those impacted, therefore 'promoting a common purpose and direction to those who contributed to it' [101].

Co-designing the change vision, creates a forum to openly, honestly and constructively discuss where the change needs to head. Engagement with the change vision needs to be active and two-way for people to truly live it and take accountability and ownership of bringing it to life.

Engagement with the change vision

After co-designing the change vision, we cannot set it and forget it in a document or on a wall; it needs to be constantly communicated and discussed as people work towards it in unison.

When I start with an organisation, I often ask people what the vision and values of the organisation are. Unfortunately, many fumble, trying to piece the vision together. A vision is only as good as how embedded it is within an organisation. Is it a statement that is too complex or dry for people to remember or is it always spoken about, gripping their hearts and minds? When people refer to the vision, is it heartfelt, authentic, and does it hit home for each person?

Another question to ask is, who is the vision communicated to? Is it only executives, is it all staff, or is it reaching customers? When everyone, including customers, knows the vision, this creates a shared sense of purpose, transparency, and the alignment needed for successful change.

Aligning with the change vision

As mentioned in chapter six, a change strategy includes a change vision, which should align with the organisational vision.

Alignment around the change strategy is vital in ensuring that each employee is involved in achieving the goals and that all activities within change implementation contribute to achieving the change vision [102]. Alignment also requires a concerted effort to help people understand the issues and their respective roles in achieving the change vision. Therefore, alignment would extend to the granular team and individual goals [103,104].

The mural that I mentioned in the previous chapter illustrated a clear alignment within the organisation's overall change strategy by depicting; where they wanted to go (their vision), what they needed to achieve (their goals and objectives), and the boundaries within which they planned to get there (their values).

We must have a change vision that inspires others and aligns with the overall organisational vision.

THE ROOT OF ALL EVIL

For centuries, people have attributed the root of all evil to one thing - money. I believe something else is also incredibly destructive to individuals, couples, families, workplaces, communities and the world...

Ineffective communication.

> *"The single biggest problem in communication is the illusion that it has taken place."*
>
> George Bernard Shaw

Types of ineffective communication and examples of their dire consequences include:

- Miscommunication - which played a prominent role in the inception of the Cold War. The American and Soviet governments could not communicate clearly on cultural and economic matters, in addition to language barriers and misinformation through propaganda [105].

- Missed communication - during the battle of Trenton in 1776, a note subtly placed in a general's pocket, revealing a hidden message of an upcoming ambush, was not read, leading to his death and defeat of his army [106].

- Misinterpretation of written communication - the Moses sculpture built by Michaelangelo, has Moses depicted with two horns on his head. There is continued debate about the horns' symbolism, however, one researcher on the topic concluded that when translating the Bible from Hebrew to Latin, the wording was misinterpreted as 'horns' instead of 'radiance' [107].

Communication is critical in all areas, at all levels and during all principles in the 6E Change Facilitation Framework. When it is clear, concise, transparent and consistent, there is no need to seek it from less reliable sources or entertain rumours and hearsay. Ineffective communication can cause division, loss in productivity, increased stress levels and loss of trust - all the ingredients to prevent successful change.

In chapter five, I mentioned working with a global organisation on its transformation. As a result of active communication throughout the exploration of their change factors, stakeholders were able to:

- Connect and empathise with one another.

  Seeing that other countries were going through the same change barriers allowed country leads to feel connected. It built their empathy and removed the competitiveness of their approach. One lead shared, *"It's nice to know that these feelings are normal and that I'm not totally crazy!"*

- Understand and make sense of their experiences.

  By understanding why humans resist change and identifying tangible change factors, they were able to finally make sense of the chaos in navigating their changes. One lead remarked, *"It's great to see that we are not alone. We do see the fight, flee, and freeze responses, and now I know why."*

- Create accountability for problems and solutions.

  Rather than have executives or consultants pointing out their gaps and faults, the country leads explored and defined their change barriers. Instead of denying or justifying their shortfalls, they were identifying and owning solutions to the barriers. This was a powerful approach to reduce potential resistance to the proposed changes. One lead shared, *"Now I realise that change is a marathon, not a sprint. I may not see the end of it, but I can take an active and positive approach to it."*

- Navigate unique cultural barriers.

  When exploring barriers at a local level, the country leads highlighted additional cultural factors specific to their regions. This opened the discussion to share their unique challenges and enable others to empathise, appreciate and learn from their differences.

In our research, Change Facilitators observed that leaders often inadequately communicated the upcoming changes to their teams. In some cases, changes in roles were not clarified or communicated early to those impacted; therefore, messages were misconstrued, leading to frustration and team breakdowns, just like what happened with Nancy.

During a significant merger of a large telecommunications company, an employee told me that very little information was communicated about the change. The merger meant many roles, particularly in shared services such as Finance,

Information Technology, and Human Resources, would eventually be made redundant, however, there had been no communication for nearly two years- since the merger was first announced. The lack of communication and clarity created an environment rife with rumours. Worse yet, when a momentous update was finally provided by leadership, it was simply sent via a broadcast email. There was no prior discussion with those potentially affected, resulting in confusion as people were left to interpret and process without sufficient channels to raise their questions and concerns. The outcome was an unprecedented increase in staff turnover.

Ironically, one of the least effective strategies in our research to address 'ineffective communication' was 'informing stakeholders of the change'. This included 'inform individuals/the entire group of the change and objectives verbally', 'inform using a visual display such as a poster', and 'inform using a written document (e.g. email)' [57].

'Informing' is a one-way method of communication. It does not guarantee that the person being 'informed' is absorbing or understanding the message, especially what the change means for them. When we simply inform, we remove the potential for deep two-way discussions, active engagement, and the 'opportunity to interact and develop a shared understanding about the process needed... to achieve the shared goals' [108].

The categories with the highest likelihood of addressing this barrier were: 'engaging stakeholders', 'empowering stakeholders', and 'equipping stakeholders'. All pertained to two-way communication and engagement.

Employees tend to be regularly informed but rarely engaged. There is no shortage in the quantity of communication channels such as emails, messages, newsletters, social media platforms, tele/video conference platforms and virtual/collaboration whiteboards. However, there is a shortage in the quality of communication through existing channels.

Figure 8.1 The effects of informing vs. engaging stakeholders during change communication

When a lack of communication is an organisational change barrier during our projects, we conduct diagnostics to determine the different communication styles within a team. These insights allow teams to tailor their communication approaches, reducing the ramifications of miscommunication, misinterpretation and breakdown of trust.

Consider many of the problems you've faced in your personal or professional life. If you dig deep enough, they evolved from ineffective communication of one sort or another.

Within a family setting, two-way engagement is also extremely important for children, especially during change. When they feel like they are part of the decision-making process, that their views matter and ideas are considered, they become more willing to go along the change journey no matter how dramatic the change may be.

Whilst all the principles in the 6E Change Facilitation Framework are valuable, if you were going to take one thing away from this book, it is to consistently engage those involved and impacted throughout the change journey.

We need to clarify and place emphasis on our communication, moving away from simply informing people about change to engaging them throughout the change journey

EASY TO BREAK, HARD TO REBUILD

Here is a riddle - what takes seconds to break and years to rebuild? It's also one of the most critical ingredients during change.

The answer: TRUST

> *"The most expensive thing in the world is trust. It can take years to earn and just a matter of seconds to lose."*
>
> Unknown.

It is so influential that the level of trust in a society strongly predicts its economic success [109]. When citizens trust their leaders, they are willing to contribute to shared decision-making through increased willingness to vote; they are also more willing to pay taxes and support their government's choices [109].

The level of trust within an organisation can also mean the difference between its success or demise. A study conducted in the United States, surveying 6,500 employees in the hospitality industry, highlighted that a one-eighth point improvement on a five-point scale of trust meant a 2.5% increase in revenue. For medium-sized businesses, this translated to a $250,000 profit increase per year [110].

Increased trust can also significantly improve innovation within an organisation [76]. When we are trusted, we are more willing to experiment, leverage our creativity and know that we are 'safe' even if we fail. Trust also correlates to improved culture, communication, transparency and reduced staff turnover [111].

There are many definitions and complex theories in the literature regarding 'organisational trust', including:

'The extent to which a person is confident in and willing to act based on the words, actions and decisions of another' [112].

'A psychological state comprising the intention to accept vulnerability [to another] based upon positive expectations of the intentions or behaviour of another' [113].

When explaining the concept of trust to our children, we distill these definitions down to something straightforward...

Trust is gained when words = consistent actions

It's when someone says they will do something and follows through. With enough consistency, trust is built and solidified. However, inconsistent behaviour breaks down trust or prevents it from being built in the first place.

Organisational psychologists have identified different types and measures for trust in an organisational setting [114]:

- Interpersonal trust - concerned with trust in people, which can be:
    - Lateral trust - is trust between employees
    - Vertical trust - is trust between employees and leadership

- Impersonal/ Institutional trust - concerned with trust people have in the vision, strategy, processes, structures and policies. This can be broken down into:
  - Situational normality - is the appearance that everything is normal.
  - Structural assurance - is the assurance that there are structures, policies, beliefs and regulations in place to ensure continued success.

INTERPERSONAL TRUST   **INSTITUTIONAL TRUST**

Why are these concepts relevant during change?

If there is no interpersonal trust, i.e. people do not trust those around them (particularly leadership), they often fall back on institutional trust, i.e. a system, structure or regulations that will ensure their safety and security. However, when there is neither interpersonal nor institutional trust, the organisation's foundations crumble, leading to low morale, reduced performance and ultimately high staff turnover.

Change is inevitable; to navigate its chaos, we need structures in place which provide assurance that regardless of the scope or leader, there will be continued success of the organisation. An adaptable organisation is built on a solid foundation of interpersonal and institutional trust, which can be achieved through constant engagement and ensuring words = actions.

A critical aspect of building trust is what we delved into in the previous section - communication - not just informing but engaging through effective two-way channels.

Another aspect is alignment, which can't be assumed simply because we have communicated the change. Alignment does not mean blind agreement, but discussing and addressing all concerns until there is consensus towards a common goal, vision, and objectives.

Misalignment often manifests in resistance symptoms like the fight, flee or freeze response. When misalignment is coupled with a lack of trust, people will likely leave the organisation or actively cause division.

Reaching alignment requires time and may be accompanied by disagreement and differing perspectives, however, it is more likely to result in a change's success than an enforced mandate.

Unfortunately, I have seen leaders enforce change mandates in many organisations and communities rather than engage and navigate disagreements directly. When those impacted do not agree, leaders replace healthy, diverse, dynamic conversations with justifications or simply ignore the opposing opinions creating further division.

Even children can no longer be appeased by the outdated response of "because I said so". As often as practically possible, Andrew and I intentionally try to explain decisions to our children and gather their input. If we go to such lengths to appease children, how can we expect adults to simply do what they are told when it is their livelihood, sense of security and duties on the line?

To build trust, leaders need to engage and address concerns. If leaders do not take this first step, employees should be able to raise their concerns to them. For employees to do so, they need well-established systems and processes, and to feel empowered to speak up, a principle we will discuss in the next chapter.

> **Trust is where words consistently match actions - when there is interpersonal and institutional trust, people will have more faith in the change.**

KEY TAKEAWAYS

- The *'Engage'* principle is the most critical within the 6E Change Facilitation Framework.

- A change vision can capture the hearts and minds of those going through the change journey, while the change goals, objectives, and measures can help bring it to life.

- By consistently embedding two-way communication, we move from passively informing others about upcoming changes to actively engaging them throughout the change journey.

- To form a solid foundation for change implementation and adoption, we need to build interpersonal and institutional trust where our words consistently match our actions.

ADDITIONAL RESOURCES

Scan the QR code at the end of the book to access diagnostics that determine your and your team members' communication preferences.

EMPOWER STAKEHOLDERS TO PLAN FOR CHANGE 09

> *We need to replace the old mentality of 'build it, and they will come', with get everyone to build it, and they will stay.*
>
> Dr Lydia Moussa

MANY MEMBERS - ONE ORGANISATIONAL BODY

When our daughter Elaria turned three, Andrew and I worked all night to revamp the playroom. We made it so pretty, coordinated and colourful. We were very excited to show it to her, so the following day, we blindfolded her and did the big 'ta-da' reveal. She went into the room, said "Wow", and walked straight back out.

Her initial reaction wasn't the problem; it was the following week when the room was turned upside down. We had printed pictures to help her identify where items were meant to go, yet it descended into a colourful mess.

Having gone through this experience, the next time we revamped the playroom, we wanted Elaria to do it all by herself - unfortunately she was not at a stage (age, height or capability) to do it alone.

Similarly, institutions can go from extremes of total control (followed by the 'ta-da' moment) to requesting that employees take complete responsibility for the change. These are referred to as 'top-down' and 'bottom-up' approaches:

- **Top-down approach** - sets out that institutions are determined by laws written by political and organisational leaders [115]. With this approach, radical changes are implemented by leaders as they control strategy and funding, however, organisational members often resist such radical changes as they have little input in their design. Therefore leaders ultimately spend more time, effort and resources to increase levels of acceptance and adoption.

- **Bottom-up approach** - views institutions as emerging spontaneously from the social norms, customs, traditions, beliefs and values of the individuals within, with the written law only formalising what is already mainly shaped by the attitudes of individuals [115]. With this approach, change tends to be initiated and driven by individuals and teams within the organisation. The change will likely be tailored to the needs of the members within the organisation and led by those impacted. However, this can take longer to gather momentum and can fail quickly if leaders are not supportive of the proposed changes.

Whilst the bottom-up approach is admirable and aims to empower those impacted, I have seen this approach do the exact opposite. In one organisation undertaking a major transformation, they had empowered teams to design and implement their ideas. One team spent months planning a new training program. After pouring significant time and energy into the design of this program, they finally presented it to the executives. The idea was sound, but the team was met with endless rebuttals and objections. Their case did not meet the strategic vision or address leadership priorities, so it was rejected.

'All-in' empowerment approach

Rather than change being initiated from only one part of the organisational body, we need a more collaborative and united 'all-in' approach. In this case, members of the organisation unite towards the same vision and are empowered to plan for and implement the change whilst feeling supported by leaders throughout the change journey.

In business management, empowerment has been described as a means to enable employees, including managers, to make decisions [116]. It offers the potential for optimising employee performance through a higher level of self-control [117]. Researchers emphasise the need to shift from controlling to enabling employees to contribute more [118]. In addition to the increased contribution, empowered employees show increased job satisfaction [119], autonomy in task completion [120], increased self-efficacy (confidence in themselves) [121], and increased adaptability [122].

An 'all-in' empowerment approach aims to help all members of the organisational body share in the responsibility of solving challenges related to change implementation and plan for how they will make the change successful and sustainable within their specific environments. This approach must be adopted right from problem finding through to solution design, implementation and ultimately, adoption, ensuring a more effective end-solution and efficient navigation through the change journey.

An 'all-in' approach will undoubtedly result in differences of opinion, however, as Beth Moore, the American author and evangelist, eloquently put it, *"Differences will always exist, but division doesn't always have to result."*

We must embrace the diversity of ideas and approaches that come with our differences, but this does not have to divide us, especially during change. When we recognise that we are diverse members, each able to contribute uniquely to the overall organisational body, we enable faster and more effective change implementation and adoption.

In healthcare practice, the concept of interdisciplinary collaboration (a collaboration between healthcare professionals across different disciplines) has significantly impacted the industry. In one case study, the utilisation of interdisciplinary collaboration across a hospital in the United States led to significant reductions in hospital infections and costs [123].

Returning to the playroom story, we used the next 'revamp' as an opportunity to learn from our mistakes and utilise an 'all-in' empowerment approach.

Firstly, we ensured our children were in the playroom with us. We asked their opinion on what toys and books they wanted to keep and upon which shelves they should go. We then co-designed a plan for keeping the room tidy and preempted scenarios that may arise, such as having their friends or younger cousins access their precious or hazardous toys, and asked them to suggest solutions. This strategy is critical as we empower others to go from problem finding to problem-solving.

This time, when we empowered our children to take ownership of planning their playroom revamp, they were much better at sustaining it. They knew where everything was because they were involved in the design, and the room was kept tidy because they worked hard to set it up themselves.

With each time, they also found it easier and quicker to revamp their playroom because they finally had the knowledge and skills to do so. In addition, by constantly reviewing what they had, they could make better decisions on what else they desired for their playroom.

We need to move away from 'top-down/ bottom-up' to an 'all-in' approach, where all the unique members of the organisational body are empowered and united towards achieving the change.

FROM POWER TO EMPOWER

What is the role of leaders and the 'ideal' leadership style during organisational change?

Leadership sponsorship

Sponsorship is a term frequently used in project governance. The Sponsor is a leader who works alongside the Change Facilitator and those involved in the change journey.

The Sponsor's responsibilities include [124]:

- 'Paying' for the project and controlling the flow of money.
- Aligning leadership and thereby creating support and engagement throughout the change journey.
- Clearing a path for success through issue resolution, prioritisation and solving resourcing challenges.
- Advocating and role modelling the change throughout the organisation.
- Making connections between the change and organisation.
- Motivating the team to deliver the vision.
- Partnering with the Change Facilitator/Project Manager.
- Providing objectivity and challenging the project.

Sponsorship is a critical success factor during change projects [124] and helps leaders become engaged and invested, empowering others to take ownership and share in the change. By working with the Change Facilitator, the Sponsor enables an 'all-in' approach to change.

A Sponsor's leadership style will significantly influence how well they actively empower their teams, with a flow-on impact on the change journey and outcomes.

Leadership styles

For decades, there have been debates on which is the most effective leadership style; autocratic, diplomatic, ideological, charismatic, transformational, transactional and servant leadership, just to name a few.

In every project, I find it useful to help leaders examine their leadership style and understand how it can impact change progress.

I often observe that the leader's personality, character, values and beliefs dictate their leadership style; meaning that the organisation, including its strategy, culture and priorities, sometimes become dependent on and strongly influenced by that leader's unique style. Whilst this can have benefits, it can also pose significant challenges during change.

For example, **ideological leaders** will frame problems through adherence to tradition, drawing allusions to highly valued experiences they share with like-minded followers [125]. Whilst this may be of benefit to keeping a long-standing organisation authentic and genuine to its roots, it can become a hindrance when change is required to adapt to an ever-changing environment. One example was Jair Bolsonaro, the President of Brazil, who insisted that COVID-19 was not a serious threat and advocated nonscientific findings to combat it. Bolsonaro's denial eventually led to a public health emergency and economic crisis [126].

On the other hand, **charismatic leaders** are future-focused and possess 'a fire that ignites followers' energy and commitment, producing results above and beyond the call of duty' [127]. However, such leaders often discount or ignore key functions for successful change, such as planning and decision-making [128]. This was highlighted by critics of Justin Trudeau, Canada's Prime Minister, who commented that despite using confident language, his actions during the pandemic suggested costly unpreparedness [129].

In a seemingly happy medium lie **pragmatic leaders**, characterised by their overwhelmingly problem-focused and rational approach to leadership [130]. Pragmatic leaders typically do not rely on emotional appeals [131] but on fixing the problem at hand. Whilst this can be effective in times of crisis, it often lacks the sense of future hope and vision that is critical for motivating and inspiring people. Such an approach was demonstrated by German Chancellor Angela Merkel, who, after significantly reducing the number of COVID-19 cases in Germany, was quoted as saying, "it is precisely because the figures give rise to hope that I feel obliged to say that this interim result is fragile" and "the best path is one that is careful, and not taken lightly" [129]. While erring on the side of caution is essential during times of crisis, a continued pragmatic approach can diminish hope and jeopardise people's well-being. Studies indicate that Germany reported a 32.3% to 36.4% increase in anxiety disorders, placing them in the top two highest categories worldwide [132,133].

I firmly believe there is no 'ideal' leadership style and agree with the research which shows that, successful leaders rather adapt their behaviour to meet the demands of their unique situation [134].

Particularly during change, leaders need to shift from dictating their approaches to tailoring them to suit their people, empower them and accommodate changing circumstances. When leaders adapt their strategies according to the environment and the individuals, employees can maximise their learning experiences and satisfaction [135].

This adaptable and empowering leadership approach is referred to as Situational Leadership.

Situational Leadership

Situational leadership theory was developed by Paul Hersey and Kenneth Blanchard in 1977 [134] and is helpful for leaders to diagnose the demands of their situation based on extensive exploration and then tailor their leadership style accordingly.

The Situational Leadership® Model demonstrates the need to tailor a leader's direction based on the type of support that employees require. The amount of support also depends on the level of change readiness that employees exhibit [134].

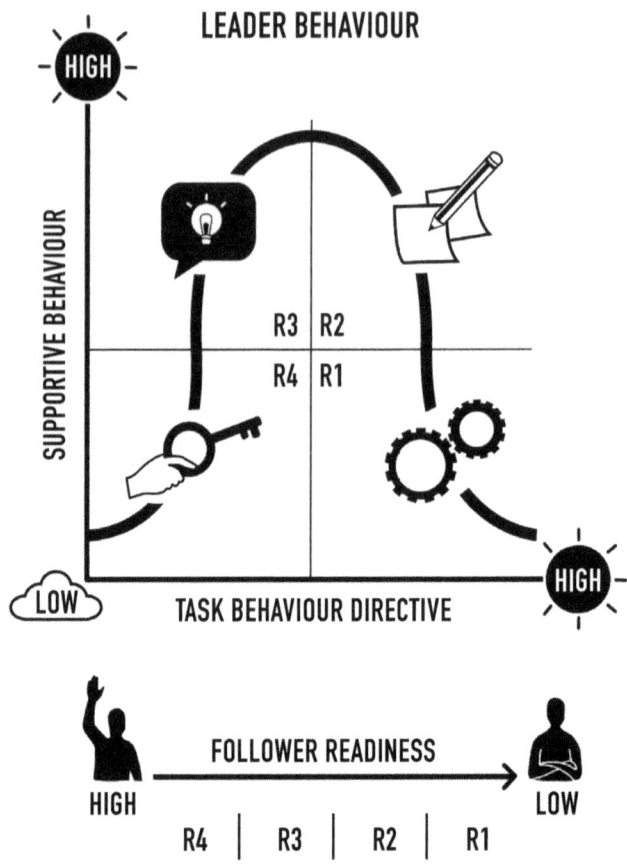

Figure 9.1 An adaptation of the Situational Leadership Model [134]

A leader must adapt their approach depending on people's readiness for change. For example, if people are unable and unwilling or insecure to implement or adopt change, the leader needs to provide specific instructions and closely supervise performance. However, if people are able and willing or confident, the leader can turn over the responsibility for decisions and implementation to them. During the uncertain days of the pandemic, countries whose leaders provided clear instructions were able to reduce case numbers significantly due to prompt restrictions and lockdowns.

Comparatively, those who did not give clear and specific instructions experienced an unprecedented increase in case numbers and a significant death toll.

Situational Leadership motivates employees and improves employee satisfaction at work [136]; increased employee satisfaction keeps people at work. Having adaptable leaders who support their people's needs is a critical asset, without such adaptability and support in the workplace, organisations exhibit higher turnover intention [137].

In addition, the 'Covid-effect' has produced a shift in the importance of certain leadership behaviours to deal with ambiguity [138] and the need for leaders to learn how to navigate the chaos of change.

Like change models, strategies, evaluation metrics, and communication styles, there is no one-size fits all leadership style. Instead, change leaders such as Sponsors and Facilitators must tailor their leadership style to navigate their people's needs throughout the change journey.

> **During change, we need adaptable leaders who tailor their approach to meet people's needs whilst being active advocates and role models for change.**

WE ARE THE CHAMPIONS

In any organisation, people are the most important asset. They know the inner workings and challenges of the business, identify workarounds to make things happen faster, maintain crucial relationships within and across teams and understand their customers best (i.e. their needs, concerns and habits).

Alongside this, some employees are more willing to initiate and embrace change than others. Categorisation of the types of adopters was shaped by Everett Rogers and George Beal in 1957 [139], graphically represented in the following Adoption Curve.

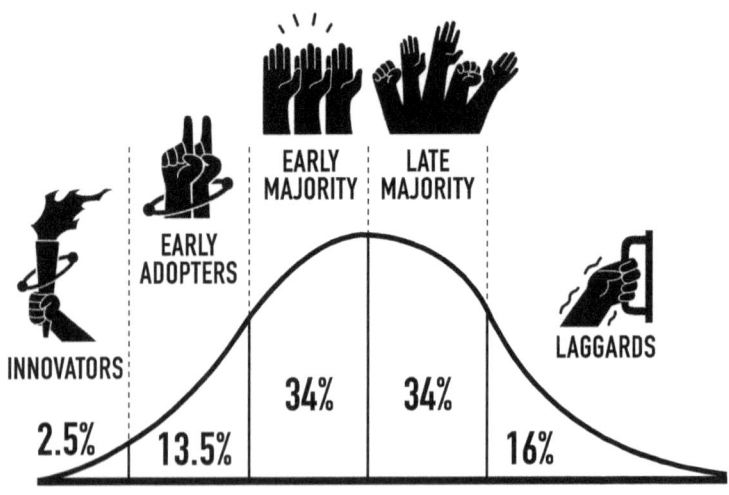

Figure 9.2 Adaptation of the Adoption Curve [139]

The types, and proportion of people who generally fit into them, include:

- **Innovators (2.5%)** - change enthusiasts who lead change and discover new ways of fixing old problems. They are typically risk takers, thrive in ambiguity and appreciate technology and efficiency. They are motivated by being change agents and often enjoy educating their peers about innovations.
- **Early Adopters (13.5%)** - visionaries who are often opinion leaders and trendsetters. They enthusiastically accept and role model change, are often competitive and want to be the first to try new things (therefore serve as excellent testers and case study creators).
- **Early Majority (34%)** - pragmatists who will go with the flow. They are willing to try something new if they know the exact benefits and trust that it will save them time, money or effort. They may not go out of their way to advocate for the change but will be willing to adopt it for their benefit.
- **Late Majority (34%)** - conservatives who may respond well to peer pressure but require more convincing. However, with sufficient facts, figures, empowerment, the building of capabilities and case studies will get on board. On the other hand, they may also be swayed to resist the change if convinced by laggards.
- **Laggards (16%)** - sceptics who are often isolated from early adopters and tightly hold onto how things were in the past. They dislike uncertainty and enjoy the security of the status quo. Whilst the fight, flee, or

freeze response to change can be displayed by all types, typically, it is most prominent with laggards.

In organisations where innovation is a core value and way of working, the proportion of innovators and early adopters is likely higher. These organisations are often new market entrants or industry disruptors. Organisations that do not frequently innovate, inadequately navigate change, or have problems with interpersonal and institutional trust, tend to have a higher proportion of laggards.

During one project, I was asked to facilitate a transformation in an organisation with a high proportion of laggards. Among the issues we had to navigate was a history plagued with a lack of structures, no follow-through from leadership and no governance or accountability. Navigating change in such an organisation requires significant upfront effort to build trust. When we built interpersonal and institutional trust, the innovators and early adopters eventually accounted for more than 30% of the organisation within two months (nearly double the average).

When navigating the chaos of change, we also need to leverage innovators and early adopters; this can be achieved through the formation of a Change Champion Network.

Change Champion Network

Change Champion Networks (also called Change Agent Networks) include members who understand the change initiative and their roles in it, the actions they need to take to implement change, and their relationships with others during the change journey. Such networks are the means through which a change initiative is accomplished well, if at all [140].

Research has also proven the benefits of Change Champions, including improving employee morale and attitudes towards change, increasing innovation and experimentation, self-organisation, and radical transparency [141].

Change Champions can help with:

- Communicating and spreading the change faster and deeper throughout the organisation.
- Testing new changes and navigating the uncertainty of new products, policies, technologies and processes.
- Providing positive and constructive feedback on applying the change within the organisation.
- Co-designing the change to tailor it to the organisation's needs, thus ensuring the adoption and sustainability of the change.
- Training and support during implementation, especially when others in the organisation trust them - saving time and money in recruiting external trainers.

In our research, we utilised the strategy of Change Champions and, combined with other strategies, improved planning for change by 84% and reduced internal resistance to the change by 78% [57]. Leveraging innovators and early adopters is helpful when building a group of champions for the upcoming change, particularly where they represent a true cross-section of an organisation and can bring unique skill sets.

Having a group of Change Champions led by a Change Facilitator and supported by a Sponsor enables a solid and collaborative network through which we can navigate change faster and more effectively regardless of the size of the organisation or the change being implemented.

As organisations build a culture of innovation and adaptability, most employees will naturally become Change Champions, and change will become a part of the organisation's day-to-day life.

A Change Champion Network can support, advocate and spread change more effectively and efficiently throughout an organisation of any size.

KEY TAKEAWAYS

- The *'Empower'* principle is critical in increasing unity, trust, role modelling and accountability during change.

- By working as one organisational (or family) body, we leverage top-down and bottom-up approaches towards a more unified 'all-in' approach to change.

- Leaders need to shift from power to empowerment by sharing decision-making and tailoring their leadership style according to the situation and people's needs during their change journey.

- To empower others and efficiently facilitate change regardless of the organisation's size, we need to leverage innovators and early adopters to form a Change Champion Network.

ADDITIONAL RESOURCES

Scan the QR code at the end of the book to access articles on the role of a Sponsor and leadership diagnostics.

EQUIP STAKEHOLDERS WITH CHANGE CAPABILITIES 10

 *Give people the right tools, and they will design and build the most extraordinary things.*

Neil Gershenfeld

SKILLS, SLEEP AND SMARTBOARDS

The 6E Change Facilitation Framework acts as a navigation system to guide our change journey through the 'destination points' of a change strategy (vision, objectives, measures). Change capabilities are also necessary when preparing for the journey, just as you would tune a car before a long trip, pack suitable clothing for the climate, research accommodation or rest before the long drive. Deploying existing capabilities while building new ones during change will allow successful strategy implementation, resulting in high growth and performance improvement [142].

According to the literature, capabilities can include, but are not limited to; resources, knowledge, skills, and capacities [143]. Using a personal example, we'll explore the repercussions of a lack of these capabilities.

As Elaria started school, the homework saga began. One afternoon she had three worksheets to complete. I was expecting a work call, so I quickly read the instructions for the first worksheet and left her to do it. Half an hour later, I came back only to find her lying on the couch without a single word written down on the paper. When I asked her why she hadn't completed the first worksheet, she promptly replied, "I can't find my pencil" *(resource gap)*. So, I brought her plenty of pencils, a sharpener, an eraser, and even tissues and water, to ensure she had all the resources she needed to complete her task.

Fifteen minutes later, I came to check on her. Whilst she made a good attempt at completing the worksheet, most of the answers were incorrect. I asked her if she had read the instructions, to which she responded, "I don't understand it, so I guessed" *(knowledge and skills gap)*. I had initially rushed through the instructions, so I re-read them, demonstrated how to do the activity and sat with her until she was confident with it.

By the time she completed the first two worksheets of her homework, with mostly correct answers, it was nearing her bedtime. I could tell she was getting restless, and her motivation was starting to plummet *(capacity gap)*. So I called it a night, and we agreed to complete the final worksheet the next day.

Resources for change

When the right organisational resources are available, teams exert more effort, show greater persistence, are more collaborative, and hence have higher levels of implementation [144]. Resources required during change can reduce the strain and stresses often associated with organisational change and fuel employees' commitment to it [145].

How do we understand what resources people need? By *'Engaging'* them through the *'Explore'* principle to identify resource gaps, and then *'Establishing'* the appropriate strategy to equip them with these resources.

Examples of resources usually required during change include; people, policies, processes, time, funding, remuneration, incentives, physical space, tools, fixtures, equipment, software and hardware.

Alongside determining the resources required to implement and adopt change, we also need to consider using existing resources. In our research, two resource-related factors were: 'resource availability' and 'resource use'. It is, therefore, useful to consistently *'Evaluate'* the use of our existing resources concerning our desired change outcomes to ensure they are not being underutilised.

Often, one of the most underutilised resources in an organisation is the human type - people. How do we invest in our most critical resource? By building their knowledge and skills.

Knowledge and skills for change

Organisational capabilities, including; knowledge, skills and experience, provide the internal dynamic behind organisational growth [146]. An essential component within this is to embed change capabilities - having the knowledge, skills and experience to navigate change creates a culture of adaptability and resilience to withstand internal and external pressures and thrive in uncertainty.

In the following two sections of this chapter, we will delve into ways to build internal capabilities, navigate the learning journey and tailor learning to suit people's needs. For now, the final question that needs to be asked is...

Are people ready for the change?

Capacity for change

With my husband's veggie patch, there have been some triumphs, such as an abundance of plump cherry tomatoes during the summer. Some lessons have also been learned, including waiting until after winter to plant strawberries. There is an optimal time to plant, and conditions must be suitable to obtain the fruits from our labour.

Not too dissimilar is the attempt to sow the seeds of change when people do not have the capacity to 'water' and 'nurture' those seeds. When change is introduced at the wrong time, it can significantly reduce productivity and overwhelm organisational members [147].

One of the critical aspects of change readiness that I measure when starting a project is to determine people's capacity for change. We measure capacity by gauging whether people are currently in their 'comfort', 'stretch' or 'panic' zones.

Whilst this is subjective according to each person's interpretation and capacity within 'comfort', 'stretch' and 'panic', that's precisely the intention. Everyone has a different size 'tank', which is filled and emptied in a way that is unique to their needs and efforts, therefore, it is vital to check in before commencing change to understand where each person's capacities lie. If people are consistently in the:

- **Panic zone** - this is a clear sign of change fatigue; at this point, further conversations around change will exacerbate the issue.
- **Comfort zone** - this signifies a lack of change and innovation, and people are likely to resist changes that push them outside their comfort zone.
- **Stretch zone** - they are continuously growing and learning, which is a fruitful foundation for change that is navigated correctly.

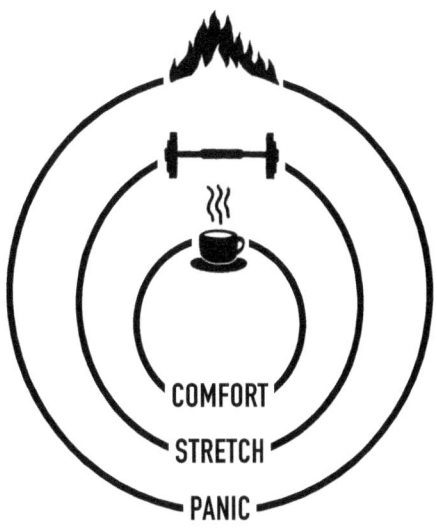

Figure 10.1 Capacities for change - adapted from Panicucci's Comfort Zone model [148].

An organisation was looking to improve their ways of working and increase collaboration. The great thing was that leadership was very engaged- there was clear sponsorship and role modelling of the change. On my first visit, I noticed a large space when entering the building. It was dark, gloomy and empty. Beyond this space were all the employee desks with partitions between each one.

My first suggestion to the leadership team was to address the *resources needed for change.* To increase collaboration and break down 'mental silos,' we first needed to remove the physical ones. We also revamped the empty space and turned it into a bright and inviting area with the resources to collaborate and innovate.

The change in space improved morale and collaboration, but we also had to address the *knowledge and skills needed for change.* We conducted workshops to determine existing learning gaps, which informed the co-design of an organisation-wide training plan, where they would learn the content and apply it in their practice over the following six months. In addition, we enabled the innovators and early adopters to form a group of Change Champions from across the organisation, to support change implementation and adoption.

Simultaneously, we worked with the entire organisation to determine and navigate their *capacities for change*. It would be futile to build capabilities or request that people utilise new resources if they did not have the capacity for change. Therefore, the leadership team needed to outline the organisation's priorities and subsequently understand from teams where their capacities lay. From this data, we created a staggered timeline that enabled us to equip employees when they reached an ideal capacity (or close to). For example, specific departments were undergoing a significant restructure, which meant that some people were taking on additional responsibilities - therefore they were last in our staggered timeline for change implementation and adoption.

We need to equip people with the resources and capabilities they need for change whilst ensuring they have the capacity to make change happen.

DRIVING THE LEARNING JOURNEY

I have a friend in her mid-twenties who has no desire to get her driver's license. She failed the driving test once and didn't bother again. To many people, that might seem absurd, but for her, there's no intrinsic motivation to drive. She lives close to a train station, works in the city, can get anywhere fairly quickly and can save money for the things she wants other than a car. The idea of learning to drive is more strenuous than the satisfaction of driving.

For me, driving a car meant I could finally go to places on my own, spend more time with my friends and gain a sense of independence. I had a lot of inner 'fuel' to push through the sometimes overwhelming experience of learning to drive.

I'd like you to think back to your fifteen-year-old self, sitting in the back seat of your family car.

You are familiar with many of the buttons and levers but not much else. Despite this, you may be getting excited at the imminent prospect of driving, thinking, "how hard could it be?"

You've now turned sixteen, passed the theory exam to ensure you know all the road rules and successfully obtained your Learner's license.

Then the moment you've been waiting for finally arrives as you sit in the driver's seat. Suddenly, you feel an odd sensation in your stomach- nerves. You realise there are many more buttons, gauges, mirrors and other settings. From this angle, everything looks very different, and it's overwhelming.

You find the resolve to finally pull the seat belt over and turn the key, only for the car to make a loud shrieking sound. You feel like you've been zapped, so you snap your hand back and look at your instructor in despair, thinking, "Oh no, I already broke it."

Does that experience sound familiar, or was it just me?

In all that excitement, I hadn't realised that I didn't know how to turn on the car.

When learning something new, we 'don't know what we don't know'. This stage in the learning journey is called **'Unconscious Incompetence'.** We might be excited, anxious or apathetic towards the change but are oblivious to what lies ahead, so our openness to change is usually neither high nor low.

As I started driving, I realised there was much more to learn. I became more aware of my ineptitude and lack of skills. This stage in the learning journey is called **'Conscious Incompetence'**. It can leave us feeling overwhelmed, causing a drop in our motivation, and our openness to change can suddenly plummet.

After a few months of guided driving experience, I gained confidence but was still very aware and intentional of every action. Movements such as checking my mirrors were calculated and almost robotic. This stage in the learning journey is called **'Conscious Competence'**. We are becoming more skilled as we apply our knowledge; are certainly more motivated but remain alert and intentional in our actions.

After what seemed like forever, I finally obtained my Provisional license and could start driving on my own. I thought less about each of those previously intentional movements year after year. Sometimes I would get to work and think, "how did I get here?" The act of driving had moved from my Orbital Frontal Cortex to my Basal Ganglia and become 'Business As Usual'. This stage in the learning journey is called **'Unconscious Competence'**. Whilst this is where we become 'experts' in a skill, it also means we can become comfortable and may not actively seek changes in this area.

These stages are referred to as 'The Four levels of teaching', 'The Four Stages of Competence', 'The Conscious Competence Matrix' or 'The Learning Curve Model'. The theory was initially founded by Martin Broadwell in 1969 [149].

It is essential to equip stakeholders with change capabilities to adopt change successfully, including building knowledge and skills. Some people may have prior knowledge or experience, which propels them faster toward unconscious competence. However, these capabilities may be entirely new for many, so a systematic and intentional journey is required to take them through the stages.

As we support people through the learning journey, we can navigate the **'unconscious incompetence'** stage by 'engaging' them early, reducing hesitance and apprehension and focusing on the new opportunities the learning will bring.

To navigate the **'conscious incompetence'** stage, we continue to 'engage' people while we collaboratively 'explore' their learning barriers, 'empower' them to 'establish' strategies, and continue to 'equip' them with the resources they need to achieve their learning goals.

To navigate the **'conscious competence'** stage, we need to 'empower' people to apply their learnings and help them 'evaluate' and celebrate their change progress. Once someone has reached a level of **'unconscious competence'**, they would have 'honed their abilities so much that it is now innate or second nature' [150].

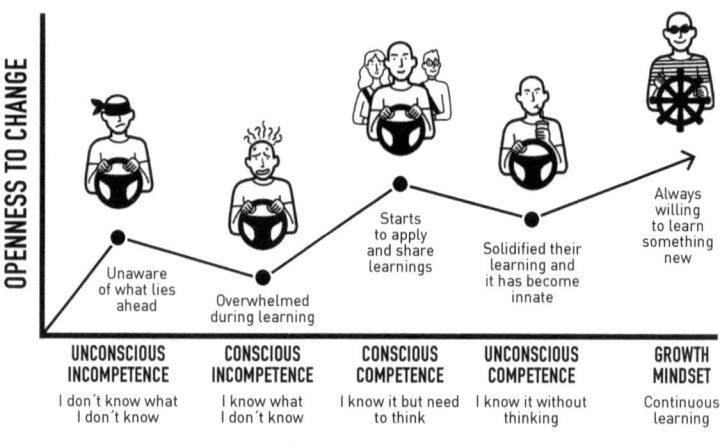

Figure 10.2 Openness to change throughout the learning journey, adapted from the Four Stages of Competence [149].

To ensure that our people remain adaptable and continue to grow, we need to embed and nurture a 'growth mindset'. A growth mindset allows us to think about our brain as a muscle that grows stronger and smarter when it undergoes rigorous learning experiences [151]. By embedding a growth mindset where there is no 'perfect' level of knowledge, we build a culture of constant yearning for learning, innovation and growth.

We can utilise the 6E Change Facilitation Framework to take people through the learning journey and ensure we nurture a culture of continuous learning and growth.

SAME SAME BUT DIFFERENT

I grew up being treated the same as my two sisters. Our parents made sure we had the same rules, were shown love in the same ways and taught the same things. I had always thought it was fair and consistent. As we got older and learned more about ourselves, we realised that we were three very different individuals with unique needs.

When my husband and I both started our careers in change, we became hypervigilant of how different people are. This includes characteristics, personality traits, motivational methods, teamwork preferences, learning, leadership and communication styles. After having our two children, these observations became further solidified as we realised they were very different and, in some attributes, the exact opposite of each other.

Same parents, same environment, but such different personalities.

Elaria is an intuitive, big-picture idealist who learns by listening. On the other hand, Adam is a detailed sensory accomplisher who learns by doing.

Such different personalities require different strategies to cater to their uniqueness. We soon realised traditional disciplinary strategies such as 'time-out' did not work with our children. Being vocal, Elaria would feel isolated and unheard, which made her temperament worse. So instead, we would spend extra time talking her through it as she would express all her thoughts and emotions. With Adam, it was more effective to do something together as we chatted, during which time he would become calm and understand the impact of his actions.

As disciplinary methods for each of our children needed to be different, so were their learning methods. As an auditory learner, Elaria needed someone to explain new concepts to her verbally, and she would repeat what she learned. As a hands-on learner, Adam wanted to figure it out with his hands, for example, counting using blocks or patterns through a Rubik's cube.

Such uniqueness is also evident in organisational settings-same environment, vision and mission, but a diverse range of learning styles.

The VARK model stands for Visual, Auditory, Reading/Writing, and Kinesthetic (hands-on learning) and was established by Neil Fleming in 1987 [152].

Many professionals and researchers use VARK to determine the learning styles within a specific industry or organisation. For example, in healthcare, there is a high prevalence of both visual and kinesthetic learners [153–155]. Such findings come as no surprise, considering the majority of healthcare professionals need to see and touch to diagnose and treat.

Visual learners

- Need to see to learn.
- Are observant.
- Like images, videos, graphs, colours, mind maps and infographics.
- Can be easily distracted and find verbal instructions challenging to follow.

Auditory learners

- Need to listen to learn.
- Are good listeners and talkers.
- Like verbal instructions, videos, songs, podcasts, audiobooks and Q&A sessions.
- Can be distracted by noise and find complex diagrams challenging to follow. Need a quiet place to learn, yet often need to hear the instructions.

Kinesthetic (or tactile) learners

- Need to move and use physical senses to learn.
- Good at hands-on activities.

- Like to do, build or touch.
- Can be fidgety, have a short attention span or get bored quickly.

Reading/Writing learners

- Need to read and write to learn.
- Good at consuming detailed written information.
- Like to take notes.
- Can find complex diagrams and brief verbal instructions challenging to follow.

What does the research say about the most common learning styles?

The VARK Institute conducted a study in 2020 to capture the learning styles of 237,537 people. Thirty-four per cent of the participants strongly preferred one learning style only. The remaining 66% indicated a multimodal preference, i.e. where they preferred multiple learning styles.

The most common single style by far was 'Kinesthetic' learning at 22.8%, with the second most preferred being 'Auditory' learning at a mere 5.1%.

The most common bimodal preferences (two styles) were the combination of 'Kinesthetic' and 'Auditory' at 11% of people, followed by 'Visual' and 'Kinesthetic' learning at 4.9%.

Interestingly, reading/writing barely got a mention, yet traditional organisational learning strongly favours written materials such as manuals and policies.

In one organisation, I was supporting their efforts to increase internal capabilities through training. The first thing I did was determine the type of learners in the organisation through a 'VARK analysis' - after which we could tailor the training methods to suit their styles. Out of 97 respondents, 43% were Kinesthetic learners, 25% Visual, 18% Auditory, and 14% Reading/Writing- very much aligned with the VARK institute's analysis.

This concept is also used in the classroom setting, especially in early childhood learning and primary school years. Unfortunately, as students grow into their secondary school years, this tailored approach is used to a lesser extent, and even less as they enter the workforce.

How do we tailor learning and should it be to each individual?

Obviously, in a large organisation, this is not feasible; which is why we generally undertake a mixed method (or multimodal) approach, where we create and deliver learning content to suit all four learning styles (something to watch, listen to, touch or test, and read). For those who take longer to go through the learning journey, we need to utilise a more tailored and focused approach, for which we can leverage our Change Champion network to do so more efficiently.

> **As we align people towards the change, we must equip them according to their unique learning needs.**

KEY TAKEAWAYS

- The *'Equip'* principle ensures we arm stakeholders with the required change capabilities, so that they have the tools they need throughout the change journey.

- Change capabilities include; knowledge, skills, and resources and being aware and mindful of people's capacities for change.

- We must support our people through the learning curve and embed a growth mindset to ensure continuous learning, innovation, and growth.

- A multimodal approach to learning is critical to ensure knowledge is translated in a way that everyone understands, and not simply apply a one-size fits all approach to learning.

ADDITIONAL RESOURCES

Scan the QR code at the end of the book to access diagnostics on learning styles and capacities for change.

PART V

THE 6E CHANGE FACILITATION FRAMEWORK

11 THE CHANGE JOURNEY

> *Change is a journey that ought to be enjoyed as we learn to unleash, embrace, and navigate its chaos.*
>
> Dr Lydia Moussa

NANCY & ADAM - REVISITED

Revisiting the story of Nancy at the beginning of the book, we'll look at how we could have utilised the 6E Change Facilitation Framework to navigate the change from the perspective of the owner of the medical centre.

Upon 'evaluating' your business success metrics, you realise that some targets have not been met as the Sleep Clinic costs are over budget, due to having two employees rather than one. So you decide to 'engage' your most experienced clinician, Nancy, to find a solution.

By proposing the problem at hand to Nancy, you ask her for solutions - an important way to 'empower' her to plan for changes affecting her. At first, she's likely to be in denial about the clinic underperforming, so you show her the quantitative data. After seeing the data, you 'explore' factors contributing to the underperformance of the clinic. She tells you that she hates computers and therefore needs another clinician to input the patient data into the system. When prompting her for a solution (taking her from problem-finding to problem-solving), she may opt to learn how to use the computer or move to a role that is purely patient-facing (no use of technology).

Together, you 'establish' a strategy where she can continue to spend the majority of her time with patients, whilst minimising the financial impact of having two people in the clinic (a win/win strategy).

Whatever the strategy you co-design, you ask Nancy what capabilities and resources she needs to be 'equipped' with to help her through this change strategy. You also check in with her periodically to 'evaluate' her progress and capacity for change. Nancy, who was thought to be the problem, has come up with her own solution, felt empowered to plan for the change, and was provided with what she needed to make the change happen. She now looks forward to progress evaluations and check-ins. Best of all, Nancy has become a champion for change.

Adam and his chicken

How did we use the 6E Change Facilitation Framework to encourage our three-year-old son Adam to be less resistant to change and open to new foods?

Firstly, we made sure that in the future, we avoided promising something we couldn't deliver. For interpersonal trust to be built as a foundation for sustainable change, our words must equal our actions. If we promised sausages for dinner, we should honour it.

In addition to interpersonal trust, we also realised that we could build institutional trust by creating a system that caters to his wants (sausage and other 'fun' foods) and our needs (healthy and diverse meals).

We started by 'empowering' Adam to plan and design this system with us. We asked our children to tell us the different foods that they like. Adam quickly indicated that these were banana bread, sausages, meat pies and noodles.

At preschool, he had been learning about healthy eating, so when prompted, he shared that there are 'all the time foods' and 'sometimes foods'. When asked about sausages, he hesitantly admitted they were a 'sometimes food'. This approach was a way to leverage the 'equip' principle and apply his learning to everyday practices.

Then together as a family, we co-designed our weekly food guide, which would be flexible and continuously updated together. The guide helped us structure our week and our children knew what to anticipate and look forward to while building their flexibility and acceptance of different foods:

- Breakfasts would be a rotation between different foods such as cereal, a sandwich and banana bread.
- Most dinners would be wholesome home cooking that Andrew and I would decide.
- At least one night, would be 'choose your own adventure' from the fridge or freezer for dinner. He could choose whatever he felt like, such as sausages, meat pies etc. This arrangement worked well for us as we had busy Thursday nights.
- Friday night would be takeaway or eating out, which everyone loved.
- Each day, we would alternate between sweets and fruit for dessert, thus applying concepts of moderation.
- The weekend remained flexible, depending on what we were doing.

Knowing that Adam is a kinesthetic learner, we introduced hands-on experiences such as using chopsticks and a knife, making him more excited to discover new foods.

Bit by bit, he became more curious and open to new foods, expanding his taste buds beyond banana bread and sausages to things like prawns, dumplings and even mussels. Acceptability and integration had been achieved, and most importantly, peace at dinner time. What was chaos was transformed into a dynamic, productive, engaging, and, dare I say, fun journey for the entire family.

The 6E Change Facilitation Framework can help us turn the chaos into an engaging transformation journey for all involved.

THE 6E'S IN PRACTICE

The 6E Change Facilitation Framework is not simply conceptual or theoretical but has been extensively utilised in research and practice.

The following outlines examples of how the 6E Change Facilitation Framework has been applied across software companies, universities and healthcare organisations.

Chatbot utilisation within universities

A software company was aiming to increase their university clients' adoption of chatbots. The chatbot was designed to answer student queries based on machine learning.

Initially, queries from students were sent to the chatbot, after which the appropriate academic would be tagged to answer the question. Eventually, the chatbot would 'learn' the answer and provide it to the next student who asks. This would eventually save the academics time repeatedly answering the same questions and help capture any consistent gaps in the curriculum.

Equip stakeholders with change capabilities

Before my engagement, the chatbot team had delivered basic technical training to the academics on how to use the chatbot.

Whilst technical training is essential when introducing new technology, it only addresses one change factor, 'knowledge and experience of the change'.

Engage stakeholders during the change journey

We organised workshops, surveys and interviews to gather feedback from each university client about using the chatbot. After analysing this information in detail, we could define some underlying change factors.

Explore change factors

- Leadership engagement and role-modelling - Some members of the leadership and academic teams were still using the old methods (Facebook Messenger, WhatsApp and email) to answer student questions rather than directing them to the chatbot.
- Lack of capacity - When prompted further, the leadership and academic teams explained that it was much easier to respond to students directly rather than refer them to the chatbot and subsequently answer the question there.
- Lack of benefit awareness - In essence, the leadership and the academic teams still did not understand or accept what the chatbot does and how it would benefit them. At this point, it was just perceived as additional work.
- Lack of trust - As the leadership and academic teams did not fully understand how the chatbot worked, they did not trust that it would give students the correct answers.
- Misaligned values and beliefs - Many academics felt that the chatbot removed the human aspect from teaching, which contradicted their belief in their role as academics.

Empower stakeholders to plan for change

Alongside the discussion of change barriers, we asked leaders and academics to highlight how the chatbot may solve some of their current day-to-day issues. Progressing from problem-finding to problem-solving, they were organically able to increase their levels of benefit awareness and trust and find an alignment to their beliefs.

Establish change strategies

In addressing the remaining change factors:

- Leadership engagement and role-modelling - we asked the leadership and academic teams how they could relay the changes in communication channels to their students. They devised several strategies, including announcing it in lectures and tutorials, creating an automated reply that refers students to the chatbot when they ask a question and sending an email to the entire cohort. They became more empowered and accountable for their change progress by coming up with solutions.
- Lack of capacity - One of the ideas was to proactively capture an extensive list of frequently asked questions and answers, which was then uploaded to the chatbot to save time and resources.

Evaluate change progress

To ensure the success of the chatbots, both the university clients and the chatbot team agreed that a live dashboard would be beneficial for continuous monitoring and evaluation of the chatbot adoption. Notably, the chatbot team involved their clients, especially academics, in the design of the dashboard to ensure the right metrics were captured.

Equip stakeholders with the right capabilities

While the academics were equipped on how to use the chatbot, my team and I ensured that the chatbot team were equipped with the tools they needed to support ongoing adoption by their future clients. We co-designed a change guide centred around the 6E Change Facilitation Framework. The guide included an extensive list of the factors explored, effective strategies established, different metrics used for evaluation, engagement and empowerment approaches, and the capabilities needed to equip their clients.

New guidelines in healthcare

To increase the adoption of new heart failure guidelines, the Pharmaceutical Society of Australia (PSA) wanted to help healthcare professionals navigate these changes and embed them in their daily practice. Healthcare professionals (HCPs) included General Practitioners (GPs), nurses, pharmacists and specialists.

Equip stakeholders with change capabilities

To provide HCPs with the knowledge and skills they need to navigate upcoming changes, we started with change training workshops. As a former healthcare professional, I recalled the lack of education around running a business or dealing with conflict, let alone navigating change. With rapid changes in healthcare, it is evident that such adaptability is critical in this industry.

Engage stakeholders during the change

During these workshops, I was able to engage participants through a variety of materials to cater for all the different learning styles. We also used the time to explore barriers preventing them from implementing the changes in their practice.

Explore change factors

With representatives across several healthcare practices, we were able to identify common change factors, which included a lack of existing processes and systems, appropriate resources, internal support for the change, and experience and knowledge among staff.

Establish change strategies

Given the variety of different factors highlighted by the group, we utilised the KJ technique (you can find out about this by scanning the QR code at the end of the book) to map out all of the possible strategies to address them.

Empower stakeholders to plan for change

It was then time to empower the representatives to plan how they would bring these strategies to life in their practices, which we also supported through six months of coaching.

Engaging different stakeholders throughout the journey enabled them to share in the decision-making process, increasing adoption and accountability. For example

- While taking blood and giving injections, **Nurses** would ask patients about any symptoms that may allude to heart disease and flag these to the GP.

- By observing the medication taken by patients, **Pharmacists** would ensure none of these would aggravate their heart condition and raise any issues to the GP accordingly.

- By asking the right questions to patients who may be susceptible to heart failure (even if they don't display symptoms), **GPs** would detect any issues early on and refer them to **Specialists**.

- By reminding patients of follow-up appointments, **receptionists and administrative staff** would promote ongoing monitoring for patients with early signs of heart failure.

Evaluate change progress

Through quantitative and qualitative measures captured in their online systems, health practices were able to evaluate progress based on:

- Number of early diagnoses of heart failure
- Number of follow-up appointments for patients with heart failure
- Number of patients who attended their appointments

Additional outcomes - a culture of adaptability

In addition to implementing the new heart failure guidelines, many practices built a culture of adaptability and resilience. In the months following my engagement, they shared images of their team facilitating co-design workshops to improve other areas in their practice - a true reflection of embedding this new culture.

The 6E Change Facilitation Framework enables us to start wherever we are in the change journey and navigate the chaos according to the needs of those impacted by the change.

THE WHOLE PICTURE

I hope this book is helpful to you as you navigate the chaos of change.

This journey starts by understanding why we, as humans, struggle with sudden change and how resistance is simply a natural response. It is a superficial symptom underpinned by complex factors that preserve our survival, sense of belonging and security.

Along this journey, we have also come to realise that 'managing' or 'controlling' change is not only ineffective but futile. Humans come with an array of underlying and individualised complexities, making their reactions to change impossible to control. This calls for a more facilitative approach that leverages their uniqueness and brings people together.

Importantly, chaos is not only inevitable but a prerequisite for true transformation. When we introduce a change, no matter the magnitude, it disrupts the status quo, leading to unpredictable reactions that seem chaotic. However, to undergo any long-term transformation, we need to unleash the chaos beneath the surface, acknowledge it, and unearth hidden talents and positive factors that we can leverage during the change journey.

We delved into the need to 'change how we do change' as an industry - shifting from linear models (the inflexible street directory) towards a dynamic (live navigation system) and tailored approach. Critical aspects necessary to combine include diagnosis/prescription and implementation/adoption, all while placing people at the heart of the change journey from inception through to embedding.

The culmination of this is the 6E Change Facilitation Framework- a navigation system to guide us through the chaos of change.

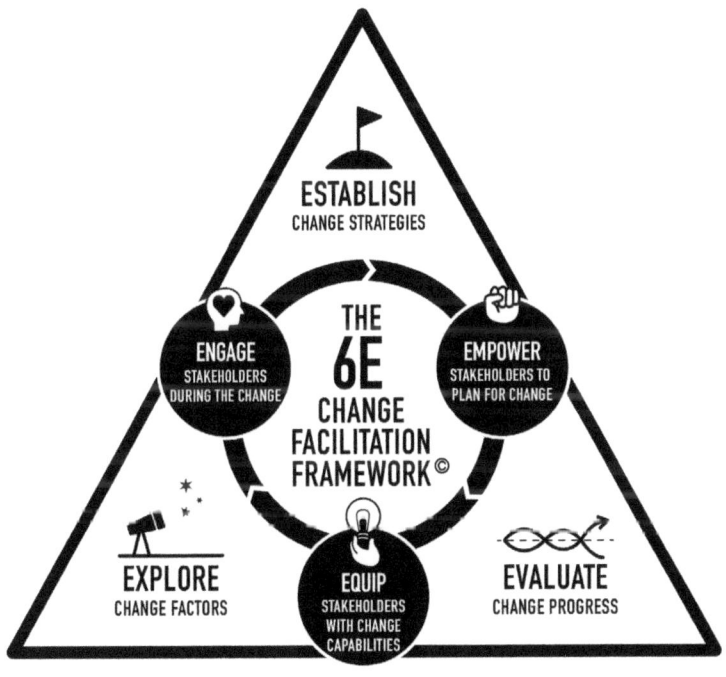

Figure 11.1 The 6E Change Facilitation Framework by Dr Lydia Moussa [58].

The triangular shape of the framework enables it to be dynamic, robust and tailorable to our needs. It does not prescribe where to start but allows us to start navigating change wherever we are along the journey. The inner circle represents an iterative approach to change and the need to continuously reassess aspects that must be addressed throughout the change journey.

Want to know if there are problems? We can start with the *'Evaluate'* principle to measure the progress of quantitative and qualitative metrics concerning the organisational/change vision, values and objectives. If there are concerns, we can *'Explore'* the possible change factors preventing and enabling progress and *'Establish'* change strategies to address these. All the while ensuring we constantly *'Engage'*, *'Empower'*, and *'Equip'* those involved.

Want to know what the problems are? We can start with the *'Explore'* principle to uncover change factors that act as enablers or barriers to the change (i.e. adequately diagnose where the problems lie) and *'Establish'* change strategies to address them, as well as *'Evaluate'* their progress. All the while ensuring we constantly *'Engage'*, *'Empower'*, and *'Equip'* those involved.

Want to know how to address the problems? We can start with the *'Establish'* principle and co-design strategies to address the identified change barrier, then *'Evaluate'* progress using quantitative and qualitative metrics. If progress is unsatisfactory, we can re-establish other strategies. If these strategies are still not leading to change progress, we can re-explore other possible change factors which are preventing or enabling progress to occur. All the while ensuring we constantly *'Engage'*, *'Empower'*, and *'Equip'* those involved.

Summarising the 6 Principles of the 6E Change Facilitation Framework

Explore change factors

In every setting, there is a multitude of factors that contribute to the entire ecosystem. Exploring these will help identify enablers or barriers to the change and thus establish tailored and appropriate strategies. The exploration principle enables us to unleash and make sense of the chaos at any level - local or global.

Establish change strategies

Establishing the right strategy involves opting for longer-term solutions rather than quick fixes. Strategies must also be aligned to the vision, values and objectives of the change and organisation whilst being measurable. By establishing boundaries through shared values, we start collaborating and uniting towards effective long-term changes.

Evaluate change progress

By using mixed method analysis composed of qualitative and quantitative measures, we tap into the hearts and minds of people.

Additionally, aiming for progress and iteration over perfection will enable us to keep pace with rapidly changing internal and external environments. We can determine whether we're on the right track or getting 'off-course' through the *'Evaluate'* principle. If we are 'off-course', there are two questions to ask ourselves - was our strategy incorrect or is the barrier we are trying to address incorrect?

Engage stakeholders during the change

This principle compels us to engage people at every point of the change journey, from inception through to implementation and embedding. It involves building an inspirational change vision (aligned with the organisational vision), values and objectives.

Rather than simply 'informing' people about the change, they must be constantly and actively engaged through two-way communication. Engaging effectively will build interpersonal and institutional trust - the foundation upon which adaptable cultures can flourish.

Empower stakeholders to plan for the change

This involves a shift from one person or group holding all the power to sharing the responsibilities and accountabilities using an 'all-in' empowerment approach to change. Change leaders (Sponsors) should ideally adopt a situational leadership style. Concurrently, the organisation leverages its most significant asset (people) - bringing together innovators and early adopters to form a network of Change Champions. All the while, an expert Change Facilitator acts as a conduit to support the change, connect people, and actively engage, empower and equip all parties.

Equip stakeholders with change capabilities

We need to ensure people are equipped with the right capabilities and resources whilst also understanding their capacities for change. It may be the right change, but not the appropriate time.

We also need to recognise that learning does not happen overnight but is a journey through which people need to be supported and guided. As we equip people through this learning journey, we must adopt a tailored, multimodal approach to cater for different learning styles, rather than 'one-size-fits-all'.

> **As we bring the principles of the 6E Change Facilitation Framework together, we have a dynamic navigation system throughout our journey to successfully *navigate the chaos of change.***

◆ VALUES

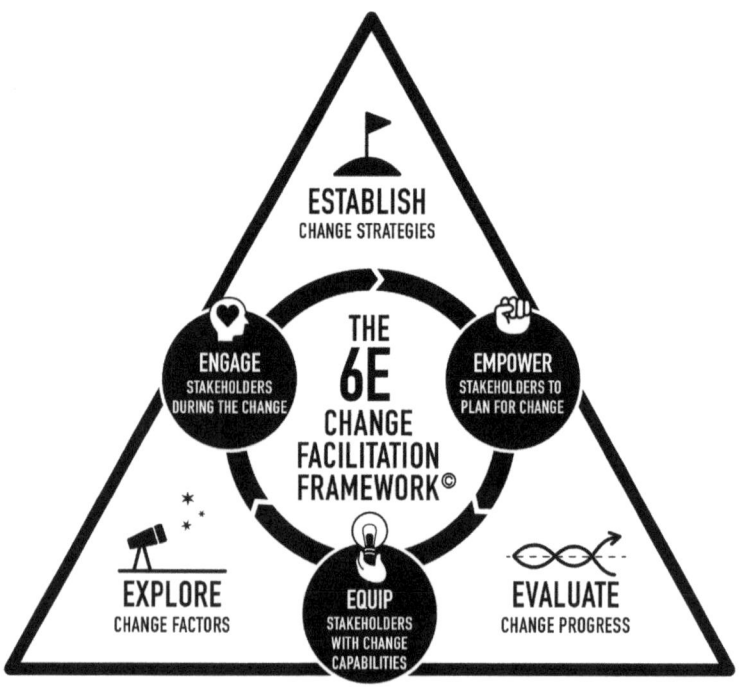

Figure 11.2 Navigating the chaos of change using the 6E Change Facilitation Framework by Dr Lydia Moussa

◆ VALUES

References

1. Carrillo JE. Industry clockspeed and the pace of new product development. Prod Oper Manag. 2009 Jan 5;14(2):125–41.
2. Cannon. Bodily changes in pain, hunger, fear and rage. ed. Appleton & Company [Internet]. Available from: https://journals.lww.com/psychosomaticmedicine/Citation/1953/09000/Book_Reviews.20.aspx
3. Scrimpshire A, Lensges M. Fear after being fired: the moderating role of resilience in lessening the time between employment. Personnel Review [Internet]. 2021 Jan 1;ahead-of-print(ahead-of-print). Available from: https://doi.org/10.1108/PR-12-2020-0860
4. Naidu G. The impact of the implementation of change management processes on staff turnover at Telkom SA [Internet]. Durban University of Technology; 2022 [cited 2022 Sep 7]. Available from: https://openscholar.dut.ac.za/handle/10321/478
5. Deutschmann A. Change or die: The three keys to change at work and in life. New York: HarperCollins Publishers Inc; 2007.
6. Kübler-Ross E, Wessler S, Avioli LV. On death and dying. JAMA. 1972 Jul 10;221(2):174–9.
7. Jang-Jaccard J, Nepal S, Alem L, Li J. Barriers for delivering telehealth in rural australia: a review based on Australian trials and studies. Telemed J E Health. 2014 May;20(5):496–504.
8. Bestsennyy O, Gilbert G, Harris A, Rost J. Telehealth: a quarter-trillion-dollar post-COVID-19 reality? 2020. Accessed December. 2020;30.
9. Chandola T, Booker CL, Kumari M, Benzeval M. Are Flexible Work Arrangements Associated with Lower Levels of Chronic Stress-Related Biomarkers? A Study of 6025 Employees in the UK Household Longitudinal Study. Sociology. 2019 Aug 1;53(4):779–99.
10. McNall LA, Masuda AD, Nicklin JM. Flexible work arrangements, job satisfaction, and turnover intentions: the mediating role of work-to-family enrichment. J Psychol. 2010 Jan;144(1):61–81.

11. Wilcox JR. Videoconferencing the whole picture. Terms, concepts, applications and interactive multimedia. New York: Telecom Books Wolcott, L (1996) Distant, but not distanced: a learner-centred approach to distance education TechTrends. 2000;41(5):23–7.

12. Panteli N, Dawson P. Video conferencing meetings: Changing patterns of business communication. New Technol Work Employ. 2001 Jul;16(2):88–99.

13. Hacker J, vom Brocke J, Handali J, Otto M, Schneider J. Virtually in this together – how web-conferencing systems enabled a new virtual togetherness during the COVID-19 crisis [Internet]. Vol. 29, European Journal of Information Systems. 2020. p. 563–84. Available from: http://dx.doi.org/10.1080/0960085x.2020.1814680

14. Resler LM. Edward N Lorenz's 1963 paper, "Deterministic nonperiodic flow", in Journal of the Atmospheric Sciences, Vol 20, pages 130–141: Its history and relevance to physical geography [Internet]. Vol. 40, Progress in Physical Geography: Earth and Environment. 2016. p. 175–80. Available from: http://dx.doi.org/10.1177/0309133315623099

15. Bronte-Stewart M. Risk estimation from technology project failure. In: 4th European Conference on Management if Technology, Glasgow, Scotland, September. 2009. p. 4–6.

16. McManus J, Wood-Harper T. A study in project failure. British Computer Society< http://www bcs Org/server php. 2008;

17. Hall ET. Beyond culture. Anchor; 1989.

18. Buono AF, Bowditch JL, Lewis JW. When Cultures Collide: The Anatomy of a Merger. Hum Relat. 1985 May 1;38(5):477–500.

19. Maslow A, Lewis KJ. Maslow's hierarchy of needs. Salenger Incorporated. 1987;14:987.

20. Lewin K, Others. Group decision and social change. Readings in social psychology. 1947;3(1):197–211.

21. Lippitt R. Dimensions of the Consultant's Job [Internet]. Vol. 15, Journal of Social Issues. 1959. p. 5–12. Available from: http://dx.doi.org/10.1111/j.1540-4560.1959.tb01442.x

22. Kanter RM, Jick TD, Stein BA. The challenge of organization change: How companies experience it and leaders guide it [Internet]. FREE PRESS,; 1992. Available from: http://www.sidalc.net/cgi-bin/wxis.exe/?IsisScript=zamocat.xis&method=post&formato=2&cantidad=1&expresion=mfn=006795

23. Kotter JP, Others. Leading change: Why transformation efforts fail. 1995; Available from: http://www.mcrhrdi.gov.in/91fc/coursematerial/management/20%20Leading%20Change%20-%20Why%20Transformation%20Efforts%20Fail%20by%20JP%20Kotter.pdf
24. Nadler DA. Champions of Change: How CEOs and Their Companies are Mastering the Skills of Radical Change. Wiley; 1997. 352 p.
25. Luecke R. Managing Change and Transition. Harvard Business Press; 2003. 138 p.
26. Hiatt J. ADKAR: A Model for Change in Business, Government, and Our Community. Prosci; 2006. 146 p.
27. Rosenbaum D, More E, Steane P. Planned organisational change management. Journal of Organizational Change Management [Internet]. 2018; Available from: https://www.emerald.com/insight/content/doi/10.1108/JOCM-06-2015-0089/full/html
28. Roberts A. Community Pharmacy: Strategic Change Management. McGraw-Hill Companies; 2007. 269 p.
29. Edward SP. Transforming library and higher education support services: can change models help? Library Management. 2008 Jan 1;29(4/5):307–18.
30. Joseph Galli B. Change Management Models: A Comparative Analysis and Concerns. IEEE Eng Manage Rev. 2018;46(3):124–32.
31. Robinson SK. A global reset of education. Prospects. 2020 Oct 1;49(1):7–9.
32. Robinson. Changing Education Paradigms: Sir Ken Robinson. (2008).[video] RSA: The Royal Society for the encouragement of Arts. Manufactures and Commerce.
33. OECD. PISA 2018 Results (Volume I) What Students Know and Can Do: What Students Know and Can Do. OECD Publishing; 2019. 354 p.
34. OECD. Correlations between spending on education and performance [Internet]. Organisation for Economic Co-Operation and Development (OECD); 2021. Available from: https://www.oecd-ilibrary.org/education/correlations-between-spending-on-education-and-performance_61a3c3df-en
35. Cooper CL, editor. McKinsey 7S model. In: Wiley Encyclopedia of Management. Chichester, UK: John Wiley & Sons, Ltd; 2015. p. 1–1.

36. The change handbook: The definitive resource on today's best methods for engaging whole systems (2nd edition). Pers Psychol. 2007 Sep;60(3):771–3.
37. Tarnow TA. Project management techniques that contribute to information technology project success in the finance industry [Internet]. 2002. Available from: https://search.proquest.com/openview/2be0eff4893debcfef2a3c81fc35cf1a/1?pq-origsite=gscholar&cbl=18750&diss=y
38. Vicente KJ. Ecological interface design: progress and challenges. Hum Factors. 2002 Spring;44(1):62–78.
39. Boy GA. Human–Systems Integration: From Virtual to Tangible. CRC Press; 2020. 240 p.
40. Patel D, Berger CA, Kityamuwesi A, Ggita J, Tinka LK, Turimumahoro P, et al. Iterative adaptation of a tuberculosis digital medication adherence technology to meet user needs: qualitative study of patients and health care providers using human-centered design methods. JMIR formative research. 2020;4(12):e19270.
41. Van Pelt A, Hey J. Using TRIZ and human-centered design for consumer product development. Procedia Engineering. 2011 Jan 1;9:688–93.
42. Stankov U, Gretzel U. Tourism 4.0 technologies and tourist experiences: a human-centered design perspective. Information Technology & Tourism. 2020 Sep 1;22(3):477–88.
43. Bevan N, Bogomolni I, Ryan N, Hirose M. Incorporating Usability in the Development Process at Inland Revenue and Israel Aircraft Industries. In: INTERACT. 2001. p. 862–8.
44. Combley R. Cambridge Business English Dictionary. Cambridge University Press; 2011. 947 p.
45. Ashkenas R. Change management needs to change. Harv Bus Rev [Internet]. 2013;3. Available from: https://www.newoaksconsulting.com/assets/docs/Change_Management_Needs_to_Change_-_HBR.pdf
46. Prosci. Best practices in change management [Internet]. Prosci; 2021 [cited 2022 Aug 31]. Available from: https://www.prosci.com/resources/articles/change-management-best-practices
47. Dogherty EJ, Harrison MB, Graham ID. Facilitation as a role and process in achieving evidence-based practice in nursing: a focused review of concept and meaning. Worldviews Evid Based Nurs. 2010 Jun 1;7(2):76–89.

48. Harvey G, Loftus-Hills A, Rycroft-Malone J, Titchen A, Kitson A, McCormack B, et al. Getting evidence into practice: the role and function of facilitation [Internet]. Vol. 37, Journal of Advanced Nursing. 2002. p. 577–88. Available from: http://dx.doi.org/10.1046/j.1365-2648.2002.02126.x

49. Baskerville NB, Liddy C, Hogg W. Systematic review and meta-analysis of practice facilitation within primary care settings. Ann Fam Med. 2012 Jan;10(1):63–74.

50. Weaver RG, Farrell JD. Managers as Facilitators: A Practical Guide to Getting Work Done in a Changing Workplace. Berrett-Koehler Publishers; 1997. 248 p.

51. Fullan M. Change Leader: Learning to Do What Matters Most. John Wiley & Sons; 2011. 192 p.

52. DA Hills. Management Fads: How to Resist Shiny Object Syndrome. physicianleaders.org [Internet]. Available from: https://www.physicianleaders.org/news/management-fads-how-to-resist-shiny-object-syndrome

53. Meadows DH. Thinking in Systems: A Primer. Chelsea Green Publishing; 2008. 218 p.

54. Arnold RD, Wade JP. A Definition of Systems Thinking: A Systems Approach. Procedia Comput Sci. 2015 Jan 1;44:669–78.

55. Senge PM, Sterman JD. Systems thinking and organizational learning: Acting locally and thinking globally in the organization of the future. Eur J Oper Res. 1992 May 26;59(1):137–50.

56. Kim DH, Senge PM. Putting systems thinking into practice. Syst Dyn Rev. 1994;10(2-3):277–90.

57. Moussa L, Benrimoj S, Musial K, Kocbek S, Garcia-Cardenas V. Data-driven approach for tailoring facilitation strategies to overcome implementation barriers in community pharmacy. Implement Sci. 2021 Jul 19;16(1):73.

58. Moussa L. Change facilitation strategies used in the implementation of innovations in healthcare practice: Doctoral dissertation [Internet]. University of Technology Sydney ; 2021. Available from: https://opus.lib.uts.edu.au/handle/10453/156121

59. Dictionary OE. Oxford english dictionary. Simpson, JA & Weiner, ESC [Internet]. 1989; Available from: https://www.secret-bases.co.uk/wiki/Oxford_English_Dictionary

60. Pollack J, Pollack R. Using Kotter's eight stage process to manage an organisational change program: Presentation and practice. Systemic Practice and Action Research. 2015;28(1):51–66.

61. Damschroder LJ, Aron DC, Keith RE, Kirsh SR, Alexander JA, Lowery JC. Fostering implementation of health services research findings into practice: a consolidated framework for advancing implementation science. Implement Sci. 2009 Aug 7;4:50.

62. Bandura A, Jacobs KJ, Elder GH Jr, Flammer A, Schneewind KA, Oettingen G, et al. Self-Efficacy in Changing Societies. Cambridge University Press; 1995.

63. Azmat F. Opportunities or obstacles? Understanding the challenges faced by migrant women entrepreneurs. International Journal of Gender and Entrepreneurship. 2013 Jan 1;5(2):198–215.

64. Dhawan N. Women's Role Expectations and Identity Development in India. Psychol Dev Soc J. 2005 Mar 1;17(1):81–92.

65. Kupferberg F. The Established and the Newcomers: What Makes Immigrant and Women Entrepreneurs so Special? International Review of Sociology. 2003 Mar 1;13(1):89–104.

66. Roomi MA. Entrepreneurial capital, social values and Islamic traditions: Exploring the growth of women-owned enterprises in Pakistan. Int Small Bus J. 2013 Mar 1;31(2):175–91.

67. Lytch. What Teens Believe. Christ Century [Internet]. Available from: https://www.religion-online.org/article/what-teens-believe/

68. Crawford RH, Mathur D, Gerritsen R. Barriers to Improving the Environmental Performance of Construction Waste Management in Remote Communities. Procedia Engineering. 2017 Jan 1;196:830–7.

69. Hofstede. Cultural dimensions. www geert-hofstede com [Internet]. Available from: https://my.liuc.it/MatSup/2016/A86047/3%20Multicultural%20schools.pdf

70. Hofstede G. Culture's Consequences: International Differences in Work-Related Values. SAGE; 1984. 327 p.

71. Blum K, Baron D, Hauser M, Henriksen S, Thanos PK, Black C, et al. Americas' opioid/psychostimulant epidemic would benefit from general population early identification of genetic addiction risk especially in children of alcoholics (COAs). J Syst Integr Neurosci. 2019 Oct 31;5(2):1–3.

72. Ballantyne JC, LaForge SK. Opioid dependence and addiction during opioid treatment of chronic pain. Pain. 2007 Jun;129(3):235–55.

73. Dobbin F, Kalev A. Why Doesn't Diversity Training Work? The Challenge for Industry and Academia. Anthropology Now. 2018 May 4;10(2):48–55.

74. Ritchie H, Mathieu E, Rodés-Guirao L, Appel C, Giattino C, Ortiz-Ospina E, et al. Coronavirus pandemic (COVID-19). Published online at OurWorldInData. org. Retrieved from:[Online Resource]. https://ourworldindata. org/coronavirus; 2020.

75. Nations U, United Nations. Remarks on the adoption of the 2030 Agenda For Sustainable Development, New York, 25 September 2015 [Internet]. 2016. Available from: http://dx.doi.org/10.18356/d30cbc8b-en

76. Ellonen R, Blomqvist K, Puumalainen K. The role of trust in organisational innovativeness. European Journal of Innovation Management. 2008 Jan 1;11(2):160–81.

77. Sullivan W, Sullivan R, Buffton B. Aligning individual and organisational values to support change. Journal of Change Management. 2001 Sep 1;2(3):247–54.

78. The University of Reading. Strategy co-alignment: strategic executive values and organisational goal orientation and their impact on performance [Internet] [dba]. Henley Business School, University of Reading; 2005 [cited 2022 Sep 7]. Available from: https://centaur.reading.ac.uk/87062/

79. Dearlove, Coomber. Heart and soul and millennial values. Skillman, NJ: Blessing/White.

80. Dunning H, Williams A, Abonyi S, Crooks V. A Mixed Method Approach to Quality of Life Research: A Case Study Approach. Soc Indic Res. 2008 Jan 1;85(1):145–58.

81. Charles CV. A Randomized Control Trial Using a Fish-Shaped Iron Ingot for the Amelioration of Iron Deficiency Anemia in Rural Cambodian Women [Internet]. Vol. 03, Tropical Medicine & Surgery. 2015. Available from: http://dx.doi.org/10.4172/2329-9088.1000195

82. World Health Organization. The World Health Report [2010]: Health Systems Financing ; the Path to Universal Coverage. World Health Organization; 2010. 96 p.

83. Chadaga SR, Maher MP, Maller N, Mancini D, Mascolo M, Sharma S, et al. Evolving practice of hospital medicine and its impact on hospital throughput and efficiencies. J Hosp Med. 2012 Oct;7(8):649–54.
84. Sheikhzadeh Y, Roudsari AV, Vahidi RG, Emrouznejad A, Dastgiri S. Public and private hospital services reform using data envelopment analysis to measure technical, scale, allocative, and cost efficiencies. Health Promot Perspect. 2012 Jul 1;2(1):28–41.
85. Park JS, Fowler KL, Giebel SA. Measuring hospital operating efficiencies for strategic decisions. Journal of business and social science [Internet]. 2011; Available from: http://citeseerx.ist.psu.edu/viewdoc/download?doi=10.1.1.1043.4751&rep=rep1&type=pdf
86. Bartuševičienė, Šakalytė. Organizational assessment: effectiveness vs. efficiency. Soc Transform Chin Soc [Internet]. Available from: https://www.academia.edu/download/58502091/examples.pdf
87. Proctor E, Silmere H, Raghavan R, Hovmand P, Aarons G, Bunger A, et al. Outcomes for implementation research: conceptual distinctions, measurement challenges, and research agenda. Adm Policy Ment Health. 2011 Mar;38(2):65–76.
88. Curran T, Hill AP. Perfectionism is increasing over time: A meta-analysis of birth cohort differences from 1989 to 2016. Psychol Bull. 2019 Apr;145(4):410–29.
89. World Health Organization. Mental Health Atlas 2017. World Health Organization; 2018. 62 p.
90. van Jaarsveld DD, Walker DD, Skarlicki DP. The role of job demands and emotional exhaustion in the relationship between customer and employee incivility. J Manage. 2010 Nov;36(6):1486–504.
91. Project Management Institute. A Guide to the Project Management Body of Knowledge (PMBOK(R) Guide-Sixth Edition / Agile Practice Guide Bundle (HINDI). Project Management Institute; 2019. 756 p.
92. Brechner E. Agile project management with Kanban. Pearson Education; 2015.
93. Schwaber K. Agile Project Management with Scrum. Microsoft Press; 2004. 192 p.
94. Wysocki RK. Effective Project Management: Traditional, Agile, Extreme. John Wiley & Sons; 2011. 816 p.

95. Spearritt. Bradfield, John Job Crew (1867-1943). Australian Dictionary of Biography.
96. Cady SH, Wheeler JV, DeWolf J, Brodke M. Mission, Vision, and Values: What Do They Say? Organization Development Journal; Chesterland. 2011;29(1):63–78.
97. Baum, Locke, Kirkpatrick. A longitudinal study of the relation of vision and vision communication to venture growth in entrepreneurial firms. J Appl Psychol [Internet]. Available from: https://psycnet.apa.org/journals/apl/83/1/43/
98. Westley F, Mintzberg H. Visionary leadership and strategic management. Strategic Manage J. 1989;10(S1):17–32.
99. Pearson AE. Six basics for general managers. Harv Bus Rev. 1989 Jul;67(4):94–101.
100. Cole MS, Harris SG, Bernerth JB. Exploring the implications of vision, appropriateness, and execution of organizational change. Leadership & Organization Development Journal. 2006 Jan 1;27(5):352–67.
101. al-Shehri A, Stanley I, Thomas P. Developing organisational vision in general practice. BMJ. 1993 Jul 10;307(6896):101–3.
102. Todd Lombardo C, McCarthy B, Ryan E, Connors M. Product Roadmaps Relaunched: How to Set Direction While Embracing Uncertainty. "O'Reilly Media, Inc."; 2017. 272 p.
103. Moorcroft R. SILOS, POLITICS AND TURF WARS: A Leadership Fable About Destroying the Barriers That Turn Colleagues Into Competitors. Manager; Telford (Feb [Internet]. 2007 Mar;29. Available from: https://search.proquest.com/openview/af3304f29507d2f1a66150d191009913/1?pq-origsite=gscholar&cbl=30377
104. Münch J, Trieflinger S, Lang D. What's hot in product roadmapping? Key practices and success factors. In: Product-Focused Software Process Improvement. Cham: Springer International Publishing; 2019. p. 401–16. (Lecture notes in computer science).
105. Melton J. The Misunderstood Origins of the Cold War. 2019 [cited 2022 Sep 8]; Available from: https://digitalcommons.longwood.edu/spur/5/
106. Cook J, Editor. WCDS History Papers. Lulu.com; 146 p.

107. Medjuck BE. Exodus 34:29-35 : Moses' "horns" in early Bible translations and interpretations. 1998 [cited 2022 Sep 27]; Available from: https://escholarship.mcgill.ca/concern/theses/gx41mm08x

108. Ogwu S, Keogh S, Sice P. Exploring mindsight via email communication in learning environment. In Academic Conferences and Publishing International Limited; 2017. Available from: http://nrl.northumbria.ac.uk/32426/1/ECEL_2017.pdf

109. Fukuyama F. Trust: The Social Virtues and the Creation of Prosperity. Simon and Schuster; 1996. 480 p.

110. Simons T. Behavioral Integrity: The Perceived Alignment Between Managers' Words and Deeds as a Research Focus. Organization Science. 2002 Feb 1;13(1):18–35.

111. Griffith J. Relation of principal transformational leadership to school staff job satisfaction, staff turnover, and school performance. J Educ Adm Hist. 2004 Jun 1;42(3):333–56.

112. McAllister DJ. AFFECT- AND COGNITION-BASED TRUST AS FOUNDATIONS FOR INTERPERSONAL COOPERATION IN ORGANIZATIONS [Internet]. Vol. 38, Academy of Management Journal. 1995. p. 24–59. Available from: http://dx.doi.org/10.2307/256727

113. Rousseau DM, Sitkin SB, Burt RS, Camerer C. Not So Different After All: A Cross-Discipline View Of Trust. AMRO. 1998 Jul 1;23(3):393–404.

114. Costigan RD, Iiter SS, Berman JJ. A Multi-Dimensional Study of Trust in Organizations. J Manage Issues. 1998;10(3):303–17.

115. Easterly W. Institutions: Top Down or Bottom Up? Am Econ Rev. 2008 May;98(2):95–9.

116. Bowen DE, Lawler EE III. The empowerment of service workers: What, why, how, and when. Managing innovation and change. 2006;33:155–69.

117. Collins D. Control and isolation in the management of empowerment. Empowerment in Organizations. 1996 Jan 1;4(2):29–39.

118. Jones P, Palmer J, Whitehead D, Osterweil C. Performance through people. Empowerment in Organizations. 1996 Jan 1;4(4):23–7.

119. Niehoff BP, Enz CA, Grover RA. The Impact of Top-Management Actions on Employee Attitudes and Perceptions. Group & Organization Studies. 1990 Sep 1;15(3):337–52.

120. Chebat JC, Kollias P. The impact of empowerment on customer contact employees' roles in service organizations. J Serv Res. 2000 Aug;3(1):66–81.

121. Conger JA, Kanungo RN. The Empowerment Process: Integrating Theory and Practice. AMRO. 1988 Jul 1;13(3):471–82.

122. Scott SG, Bruce RA. Determinants of Innovative Behavior: A Path Model of Individual Innovation in the Workplace. AMJ. 1994 Jun 1;37(3):580–607.

123. Jain M, Miller L, Belt D, King D, Berwick DM. Decline in ICU adverse events, nosocomial infections and cost through a quality improvement initiative focusing on teamwork and culture change. Qual Saf Health Care. 2006 Aug;15(4):235–9.

124. Bryde D. Perceptions of the impact of project sponsorship practices on project success. Int J Project Manage. 2008 Nov 1;26(8):800–9.

125. Hunter ST, Bedell-Avers KE, Mumford MD. Impact of situational framing and complexity on charismatic, ideological and pragmatic leaders: Investigation using a computer simulation. Leadersh Q. 2009 Jun 1;20(3):383–404.

126. Malta M, Murray L, da Silva CMFP, Strathdee SA. Coronavirus in Brazil: The heavy weight of inequality and unsound leadership. EClinicalMedicine. 2020 Aug;25:100472.

127. Klein KJ, House RJ. On fire: Charismatic leadership and levels of analysis. Leadersh Q. 1995 Jun 1;6(2):183–98.

128. Yukl G. An evaluation of conceptual weaknesses in transformational and charismatic leadership theories. Leadersh Q. 1999 Jun 1;10(2):285–305.

129. Crayne MP, Medeiros KE. Making sense of crisis: Charismatic, ideological, and pragmatic leadership in response to COVID-19. Am Psychol. 2021 Apr;76(3):462–74.

130. Mumford MD. Pathways to outstanding leadership: A comparative analysis of charismatic, ideological, and pragmatic leaders. Psychology Press; 2006.

131. Hunter ST, Cushenbery L, Thoroughgood C, Johnson JE, Ligon GS. First and ten leadership: A historiometric investigation of the CIP leadership model. Leadersh Q. 2011 Feb 1;22(1):70–91.

132. Santomauro DF, Mantilla Herrera AM, Shadid J, Zheng P, Ashbaugh C, Pigott DM, et al. Global prevalence and burden of depressive and anxiety disorders in 204 countries and territories in 2020 due to the COVID-19 pandemic. Lancet. 2021 Nov 6;398(10312):1700–12.

133. Benke C, Autenrieth LK, Asselmann E, Pané-Farré CA. Lockdown, quarantine measures, and social distancing: Associations with depression, anxiety and distress at the beginning of the COVID-19 pandemic among adults from Germany. Psychiatry Res. 2020 Nov;293:113462.

134. Hersey P, Blanchard KH. Situational leadership. In: Dean's Forum. Citeseer; 1997. p. 5.

135. Walls. The value of situational leadership. : the journal of the Community Practitioners'& Health ... [Internet]. Available from: http://nrl.northumbria.ac.uk/id/eprint/38415/1/Walls%20-%20 The%20Value%20of%20Situational%20Leadership.pdf

136. Schweikle N. Situational Leadership : How to effectively lead and motivate employees through each development stage [Internet]. Centria ammattikorkeakoulu (Keski-Pohjanmaan ammattikorkeakoulu); 2014 [cited 2022 Aug 27]. Available from: https://www.theseus.fi/handle/10024/82414

137. Lee PC, Xu ST, Yang W. Is career adaptability a double-edged sword? The impact of work social support and career adaptability on turnover intentions during the COVID-19 pandemic. Int J Hosp Manage. 2021 Apr;94:102875.

138. Claus L. Do we need a new leadership paradigm due to covid-19? International Journal of Business and Management Research. 2021 May 22;9(2):162–7.

139. Rogers EM, Beal GM. The importance of personal influence in the adoption of technological changes. Soc Forces. 1958 May 1;36(4):329–35.

140. Bartunek JM. Organizational and educational change: The life and role of a change agent group [Internet]. [cited 2022 Aug 12]. Available from: http://dx.doi.org/10.4324/9781410606204/ organizational-educational-change-jean-bartunek

141. Battilana J, Casciaro T. The network secrets of great change agents. Harv Bus Rev. 2013 Jul;91(7-8):62–8, 132.

142. Zafer Acar A, Zehir C. Development and Validation of a Multidimensional Business Capabilities Measurement Instrument. Journal of Transnational Management. 2009 Aug 26;14(3):215–40.
143. Brits JP, Botha G, Herselman M. Conceptual framework for modeling business capabilities. In: Proceedings of the 2007 InSITE Conference [Internet]. Informing Science Institute; 2007 [cited 2022 Sep 29]. Available from: http://proceedings.informingscience.org/InSITE2007/InSITE07p151-170Brits297.pdf?ref=theredish.com/web
144. Weiner BJ. A theory of organizational readiness for change. Implement Sci. 2009 Oct 19;4:67.
145. Shin J, Taylor MS, Seo MG. Resources for Change: the Relationships of Organizational Inducements and Psychological Resilience to Employees' Attitudes and Behaviors toward Organizational Change. AMJ. 2012 Jun 1;55(3):727–48.
146. Davies A, Brady T. Organisational capabilities and learning in complex product systems: towards repeatable solutions. Res Policy. 2000 Aug 1;29(7):931–53.
147. Buono, Kerber. Intervention and organizational change: Building organizational change capacity. EBS Review [Internet]. Available from: https://www.researchgate.net/profile/Kenneth-Kerber/publication/281178734_Intervention_and_Organizational_Change_Building_Organizational_Change_Capacity/links/55da39f708ae9d659491ed12/Intervention-and-Organizational-Change-Building-Organizational-Change-Capacity.pdf
148. Panicucci. Cornerstones of adventure education. Adventure education: Theory and applications [Internet]. Available from: https://www.cabdirect.org/cabdirect/abstract/20073088306
149. Broadwell. Teaching for learning (XVI). The Gospel Guardian [Internet]. Available from: https://edbatista.typepad.com/files/teaching-for-learning-martin-broadwell-1969-conscious-competence-model.pdf
150. Keeley C. Conscious competence model and medicine. Foot & Ankle Surgery: Techniques, Reports & Cases [Internet]. 2021;1(3). Available from: https://www.fastracjournal.org/article/S2667-3967(21)00053-7/abstract

151. Aronson J, Fried CB, Good C. Reducing the Effects of Stereotype Threat on African American College Students by Shaping Theories of Intelligence. J Exp Soc Psychol. 2002 Mar 1;38(2):113–25.
152. Fleming, Mills. Helping students understand how they learn. teach profr.
153. James S, D'Amore A, Thomas T. Learning preferences of first year nursing and midwifery students: utilising VARK. Nurse Educ Today. 2011 May;31(4):417–23.
154. Kamal I, Abdul Karim MK, Awang Kechik MM, Ni X, Abdul Razak HR. Evaluation of healthcare science student learning styles based VARK analysis technique. Educ Res Eval. 2021 Mar 1;10(1):255.
155. Stirling BV, Alquraini WA. Using VARK to assess Saudi nursing students' learning style preferences: Do they differ from other health professionals? J Taibah Univ Med Sci. 2017 Apr;12(2):125–30.

ADDITIONAL CHANGE RESOURCES

Scan the below QR code to access change insights, diagnostics, videos, podcasts, articles and more.

www.thechangehub.com.au/change-resources

info@thechangehub.com.au

www.ingramcontent.com/pod-product-compliance
Lightning Source LLC
Chambersburg PA
CBHW040240010526
44107CB00065B/2817